訓練聽力　增加字彙

　　英語聽力是學習英語的重要一環，必須提早開始，長期訓練。而且要有計畫的反覆練習，絕不能只學聽單字認圖片，一定要聽句子，而且要逐漸拉長句子的內容，才能學習到英語的真諦。

　　本書是針對七、八、九年級學生的程度，循序漸進，逐步加強，期望能在 12 年國教的會考及特色招生考試中，一舉拿下聽力的滿分。本書的另一特色為在快樂學習中增加單字的記憶和使用能力，透過反覆的聽力訓練，不但大量增加字彙的累積，在不知不覺中也學會了說與寫的能力，可謂一舉數得，而且輕鬆易得。

　　為減輕學生的聽力障礙，本書將考題敘述的每個句子及答案，都精心譯為中文，以供學生參考。

　　在英語聽力測驗的出題「考點」中，我們歸納出下列幾個重點，請同學特別注意：

1. 隨時注意 7 個 W：who, when, what, where, which, why, how
　　　也就是人、時、事、地、物、原因、狀態

2. 能夠與不能 (ability and inability)
　　　常用字詞有：can, be able to, could, can't, couldn't, not be able to, neither

1)　　A: How many languages can you speak?
　　　B: I can/am able to speak three languages fluently.
　　　翻譯：A：你能說幾種語言？
　　　　　　B：我能流利的說三種語言。

2)　　A: Has he bought a new house?
　　　B: No. He's never been able to save money.
　　　翻譯：A：他買新房子了嗎？
　　　　　　B：不，他永遠沒有能力存錢。

3)　　A: I couldn't do the homework. It was too difficult.
　　　B: Neither could I.
　　　翻譯：A：我不會做作業。太難了。
　　　　　　B：我也不會。

3. 勸告與建議 (advice and suggestion)
　　　常用字詞有：had better, I think, let's, OK, yes, good idea, sure, why not,

1)　　A: I've got a headache today.
　　　B: You'd better go to see the doctor./I think you should go to see the doctor.
　　　翻譯：A：我今天頭痛。
　　　　　　B：你最好去看醫生。我想你應該去看醫生。

2)　　A: I've got a terrible stomachache.

B: You'd better not go on working.

A: OK./All right./Thank you for your advice.

翻譯：A：我的胃痛死了。

B：你最好不要上班。

C：好的/沒問題/謝謝你的勸告。

3)　A: Let's go, shall we?

B: Yes, let's./I'm afraid it's too early.

翻譯：A：我們走吧，要不要？

B：好，走吧。/我怕太晚了。

4)　A: What/How about going fishing now?

B: That's a good idea./That sounds interesting./Sure. Why not?

翻譯：A：現在去釣魚怎麼樣？

B：好主意。/聽起來很有趣。/當然，有何不可？

5)　A: Let's go to the concert.

B: I don't feel like it. Why don't we go to the beach instead?

翻譯：A：我們去聽音樂會吧。

B：我不想去。我們為什麼不去海邊？

4. 同意與不同意 (agreement and disagreement)

常用字詞有：I think so. I hope so. I don't think so. I agree. I don't agree. So can I. Me too. Neither can I. I can't, either.

1)　A: The book is interesting.

B: I think so, too.

翻譯：A：這本書很有趣。

B：我也這麼想。

2)　A: Do you think people will be able to live on the moon in the future?

B: I hope so, but I don't think so.

翻譯：A：你認為人類將來能住到月球上嗎？

B：希望如此，但我不認為能夠。

3)　A: This lesson is interesting, isn't it?

B: I don't think so./I'm afraid I can't agree with you./I'm afraid I don't quite agree with you./I'm afraid it isn't.

翻譯：A：這堂課很有趣，不是嗎？

B：我不這樣認為。恐怕我無法同意你。我恐怕不十分同意你。恐怕不是這樣。

4)　A: I can swim well.

B: So can I./Me too.

翻譯：A：我很會游泳。

B：我也是。

5) A: I can't play the guitar.

B: Neither can I./I can't, either.

翻譯：A：我不會彈吉他。

B：我也不會。

5. 道歉（Apology）

常用字詞有：Sorry. I'm sorry about ....

A: Sorry./I'm terribly sorry about that.

B: That's all right./Never mind./Don't worry.

翻譯：A：抱歉。關於那件事我非常抱歉。

B：沒關係。不要放在心上。不要擔心。

6. 讚賞（Appreciation）

常用字詞有：That's a good idea. That sounds interesting. Fantastic! Amazing! Well done ! That's wonderful.

1) A: I've got the first prize.

B: Well done ! /You deserved to win./That's wonderful news.

翻譯：A：我得第一名。

B：真棒。你實至名歸。真是個棒消息。

2) A: We had a surprise birthday party on Saturday afternoon.

B: That was a super afternoon.

翻譯：A：星期六下午的生日聚會令人驚喜。

B：那是個超棒的下午。

3) A: He broke the world record for the two mile run.

B: Fantastic!/Amazing!

翻譯：A：他在兩英哩賽跑打破世界紀錄。

B：了不起。又驚又喜。

7. 肯定與不肯定（certainty and uncertainty）

常用字詞有：sure, not sure, perhaps, maybe, possible, possibly,

1) A: Are you sure?

B: Yes, I am./No, I'm not.

翻譯：A：你確定嗎？

B：是的，我確定。不，我不確定。

2)   A: When will Mary go to school?

B: Perhaps/Maybe she'll go at eight.

翻譯：A：Mary 何時上學？

B：或許 8 歲。

3)   A: His ambition is to be an architect.

B: He'll possibly go to university after he leaves school.

翻譯：A：他的願望是當建築師。

B：他離開學校後可能要念大學。

8. 比較 (Comparison)

常用字詞有：as…as…, not so… as…, more… than…, less…than…,

1)   A: How tall is Sue?

B: 1.6 meters. She's not so tall as Jane.

A: What about Mary?

B: She's as tall as Sue.

翻譯：A：Sue 身高多少。

B：160 公分。她不像 Jane 那麼高。

A：那 Mary 呢？

B：她跟 Sue 一樣高。

2)   A: Which is more important, electricity or water?

B: It's hard to say.

翻譯：A：哪個比較重要，水還是電？

B：很難說。

9. 關心 (Concern)

常用字詞有：Is anything wrong? What's the matter? What's wrong with ….?
What's the matter with ….? How's ……?

1)   A: What's wrong with you?/What's the matter with you?

B: I've got a cold.

翻譯：A：你怎麼了？

B：我感冒了。

2)   A: How's your mother?

B: She's worse than yesterday.

A: I'm sorry to hear that. Don't worry too much. She'll get better soon.

翻譯：A：令堂狀況如何。

B：她比昨天更糟了。

> A：我聽了很遺憾。不用太擔心。她很快就會好一些。

4)　A: What's the matter?

　　B: I can't find my car key.

　　翻譯：A：發生甚麼事？

　　　　　B：我找不到汽車鑰匙。

10. 詢問 (Inquiries)

常用字詞有：How, when, where, who, why, what

1)　A: Excuse me, how can I get to the railway station?

　　B: Take a No. 41 bus.

　　翻譯：A：對不起，要如何到火車站去？

　　　　　B：搭 41 號公車。

2)　A: Excuse me. When does the next train leave for Kaohsuing?

　　B: 10 a.m.

　　翻譯：A：對不起。去高雄的下一班火車是甚麼時候？

　　　　　B：上午十點。

3)　A: What's the weather like today?

　　B: It'll rain this afternoon.

　　翻譯：A：今天天氣如何？

　　　　　B：下午會下雨。

4)　A: How far is your home from the school?

　　B: Five minutes by bike.

　　翻譯：A：你家距離學校有多遠？

　　　　　B：騎單車 5 分鐘。

11. 意向 (Intentions)

常用字詞有：I'd like ..., Would you like to...? What do you want ...?

1)　A: What do you want to be in the future?

　　B: I want to be a businessman.

　　翻譯：A：你將來想當甚麼？

　　　　　B：我想當生意人。

2)　A: Would you like to work at the South Pole in the future?

　　B: Yes, we'd love to.

　　翻譯：A：你將來喜歡在南極工作嗎？

　　　　　B：是的，我會喜歡。

3)　A: I'd like fried eggs with peas and pork, too.

　　B: OK.

> 翻譯：A：我想要豆子、豬肉炒蛋。
>
> B：沒問題。

12. 喜歡、不喜歡/偏愛 (Likes, dislikes and preferences)

常用字詞有：like, dislike, prefer, enjoy

1) A: Which kind of apples do you prefer, red ones or green ones?

B: Green ones.

翻譯：A：你比較喜歡哪一種蘋果，紅的還是綠的？

B：綠的。

2) A: Do you enjoy music or dance?

B: I enjoy music.

翻譯：A：你喜歡音樂還是跳舞？

B：我喜歡音樂。

3) A: How did you like the play?

B: It was wonderful.

翻譯：A：這齣戲你覺得如何？

B：很棒。

13. 提供 (Offers)

常用字詞有：Can I ....? Let me .... What can I ...? Would you like ...?

1) A: Can I help you?

B: Yes, please.

翻譯：A：可以幫你忙嗎？

B：是的，謝謝。

2) A: Let me help you.

B: Thanks.

翻譯：A：我來幫你忙。

B：謝謝。

3) A: Would you like a drink?

B: That's very kind of you.

翻譯：A：要來杯飲料嗎？

B：你真好意。

4) A: Shall I get a trolley for you?

B: No, thanks.

翻譯：A：要我拿輛手推車給你嗎？

B：不用，謝謝。

十二年國教特色招生及會考

全新英語聽力測驗
〔八年級／高階版（下）〕

目　次

夏朵英文

國中全新英語聽力測驗試題

Unit 1

Ⅰ、Listen and choose the right picture.（根據你所聽到的內容，選出相應的圖片。）（6分）

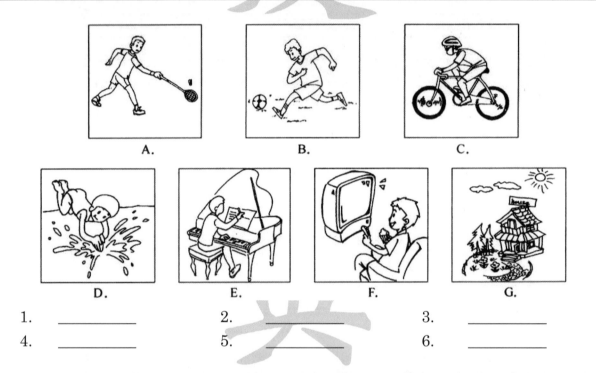

A.   B.   C.

D.   E.   F.   G.

1. _____   2. _____   3. _____
4. _____   5. _____   6. _____

Ⅱ、Listen to the dialogue and choose the best answer to the question you hear.（根據你所聽到的對話和問題，選出最恰當的答案。）（10分）

(　) 7. (A)John's family is bigger.　　　(B)John's family is smaller.
　　　　(C)Kate's family is bigger.　　　(D)Kate's family is smaller.

(　) 8. (A)Yes, I am.　　(B)Yes, she is.　　(C)No, I'm not.　　(D)No, she isn't.

(　) 9. (A)Football.　　(B)Swimming.　　(C)Tennis.　　(D)Table tennis.

(　) 10. (A)They are in a clothes shop.　　(B)They are at the fruit stall.
　　　　(C)They are in the cinema.　　　(D)They are at the hospital.

(　) 11. (A)He was travelling there.　　　(B)He had a meeting there.
　　　　(C)He went to meet the woman there.　(D)He visited some relatives there.

(　) 12. (A)Yes, he will.　　(B)No, he won't.　　(C)Yes, he did.　　(D)No, he didn't.

(　) 13. (A)He advised her to take her raincoat with her.
(B)He advised her to take her umbrella with her.
(C)He advised her not to take her umbrella with her.
(D)He advised her not to take her raincoat with her.

(　) 14. (A)Noise pollution. 　　　　　(B)Air pollution.
(C)Water pollution 　. 　　　　(D)Land pollution.

(　) 15. (A)At the boy's flat. 　　　　(B)At the girl's flat.
(C)At the cinema. 　　　　　(D)At his own home.

(　) 16. (A)Brother and sister. 　　　(B)Father and daughter.
(C)Son and mother. 　　　　(D)Workmates.

Ⅲ、Listen to the letter and decide whether the following statements are True (T) or False (F). （判斷下列句子是否符合你所聽到的信件的內容，符合的用 T 表示，不符合的用 F 表示。）（7 分）

(　) 17. Kitty receives a letter from Kelly.

(　) 18. Sally, who stands on the right of Kitty, is from the UK.

(　) 19. Kelly usually plays table tennis with Alice at school.

(　) 20. Danny can draw very well.

(　) 21. Peter practises playing tennis every day.

(　) 22. Bill is quite good at sports.

(　) 23. Kitty wants to know something about Kelly's friends.

Ⅳ、Listen to the passage and fill in the blanks. （根據你聽到的短文，完成下列內容，每空格限填一詞。）（7 分）

- Jane is __24__ years old.

- Jane is __25__ centimetres tall.

- Jane has __26__ hair.

- Jane speaks English and she can speak a little __27__.

- Jane's parents work as __28__.

- Jane's sister, Helen is an __29__.

- Jane is __30__ the floor in the classroom.

24. _____ 　　25. _____ 　　26. _____ 　　27. _____

28. _____ 　　29. _____ 　　30. _____

夏朵英文
國中全新英語聽力測驗試題
Unit 2

Ⅰ、**Listen and choose the right picture.**（根據你所聽到的內容，選出相應的圖片。）（6分）

A.　　　　　　　　B.　　　　　　　　C.

D.　　　　　　　　E.　　　　　　　　F.　　　　　　　　G.

1. _____　　2. _____　　3. _____

4. _____　　5. _____　　6. _____

Ⅱ、**Listen to the dialogue and choose the best answer to the question you hear.**（根據你所聽到的對話和問題，選出最恰當的答案。）（10分）

（　）7. (A)Before 3.15.　　(B)At 3.30.　　(C)At 3.15.　　(D)At 3.50.

（　）8. (A)The girl's.　　　　　　　　(B)The boy's.
　　　　　(C)The doctor's.　　　　　　(D)Someone else's.

（　）9. (A)Chinese and physics.　　　　(B)English and music.
　　　　　(C)History and music.　　　　(D)English and history.

（　）10. (A)By plane.　　(B)By car.　　(C)By train.　　(D)By ship.

（　）11. (A)A manager.　　　　　　　(B)A businesswoman.
　　　　　 (C)A pilot.　　　　　　　　(D)An airhostess.

(　　) 12. (A)About two weeks.　　　　　　(B)About three weeks.
　　　　 (C)About four weeks.　　　　　 (D)About five weeks.

(　　) 13. (A)At 2.55.　　(B)At 1.55.　　(C)At 2.40.　　(D)At 1.40.

(　　) 14. (A)In a library.　　　　　　　(B)In a book shop.
　　　　 (C)In a reading room.　　　　 (D)In the man's home.

(　　) 15. (A)By bus.　　(B)By bike.　　(C)By underground. (D)By train.

(　　) 16. (A)No, he can't.　(B)Yes, he can.　(C)No, he couldn't.　(D)Yes, he could.

Ⅲ、Listen to the passage and decide whether the following statements are True (T) or False (F). (判斷下列句子是否符合你所聽到的短文內容，符合的用 T 表示，不符合的用 F 表示。)（7分）

(　　) 17. Angela has got a penfriend in Australia.

(　　) 18. Spring in Canberra lasts for about four months.

(　　) 19. Summer in Canberra usually starts at the beginning of February.

(　　) 20. Judy enjoys going to the sea in summer.

(　　) 21. Judy doesn't talk much about autumn in Canberra in her letter.

(　　) 22. Winter in Canberra is always rainy and cold.

(　　) 23. Judy's favourite season is spring.

Ⅳ、Listen to the passage and fill in the blanks. (根據你聽到的短文，完成下列內容，每空格限填一詞。)（7分）

- Anita __24__ up at 6 a.m.
- After doing some washing, she __25__ English for half an hour.
- At 26, she has breakfast.
- At 8 a.m., she __27__ to school.
- At 4 p.m., she __28__ home.
- At __29__, she begins to do her homework.
- At 9 p.m., she goes to __30__.

24. _____　　25. _____　　26. _____　　27. _____
28. _____　　29. _____　　30. _____

夏朵英文

國中全新英語聽力測驗試題

Unit 3

Ⅰ、Listen and choose the right picture.（根據你所聽到的內容，選出相應的圖片。）（6分）

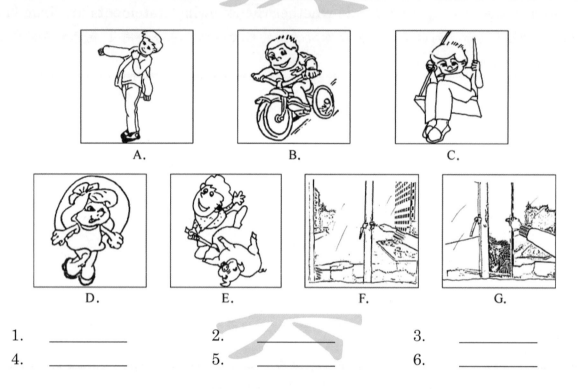

A. B. C.

D. E. F. G.

1. _____ 2. _____ 3. _____
4. _____ 5. _____ 6. _____

Ⅱ、Listen to the dialogue and choose the best answer to the question you hear.（根據你所聽到的對話和問題，選出最恰當的答案。）（10分）

(　) 7. (A)At the corner of the street.　(B)At the end of the street.
　　　(C)At the No. 48 bus stop.　(D)The lady has no idea.

(　) 8. (A)A blue handbag.　(B)A brown handbag.
　　　(C)13 dollars.　(D)30 dollars.

(　) 9. (A)Physics.　(B)English.　(C)Maths.　(D)Chemistry.

(　) 10. (A)A No. 49 bus.　(B)The bus stop.　(C)The post office.　(D)A street.

(　) 11. (A)John and Ellen.　(B)Miss Gray and Mrs Smith.
　　　(C)Mr Smith and Miss Gray.　(D)John and Gray.

( ) 12. (A)He watched TV at home. (B)He went to see a film.
(C)He visited the photo show. (D)He visited the flower show.

( ) 13. (A)She gave it to Jim. (B)She put it on the desk.
(C)She put it in the desk drawer (D)She didn't see it.

( ) 14. (A)Because the restaurant is new. (B)Because they enjoy fast food.
(C)Because the food there is not expensive.
(D)Because they are hungry and want to have lunch there.

( ) 15. (A)By train. (B)By plane.
(C)In about two hours. (D)Before three o'clock.

( ) 16. (A)America. (B)Australia. (C)France. (D)Japan.

Ⅲ、Listen to the passage and decide whether the following statements are True (T) or False (F).（判斷下列句子是否符合你所聽到的短文內容，符合的用 T 表示，不符合的用 F 表示。）（7分）

( ) 17. There is a lecture on Wednesday evening and another lecture on Thursday evening.

( ) 18. The Wednesday's lecture is about how to protect eyesight.

( ) 19. Nancy is sure that Henry will be glad to listen to the lecture.

( ) 20. Nancy was late for the lecture.

( ) 21. The ticket-collector was a very kind man.

( ) 22. Nancy and Henry are not allowed to enter because they are late.

( ) 23. It seems that Nancy doesn't remember things very well.

Ⅳ、Listen to the passage and fill in the blanks.（根據你聽到的短文，完成下列內容，每空格限填一詞。）（7分）

● Someone sent Eddie a long and __24__ package with pink paper outside. It was an __25__.

● Someone sent Eddie a square package with __26__ paper outside and a book inside.

● Eddie also received a globe of the world packed in a big, __27__ package with yellow paper from his __28__.

● Eddie received a portable computer packed with __29__ boxes in green, red and blue paper from his __30__.

24. _____ 25. _____ 26. _____ 27. _____

28. _____ 29. _____ 30. _____

夏朵英文
國中全新英語聽力測驗試題
Unit 4

I、Listen and choose the right picture.（根據你所聽到的內容，選出相應的圖片。）（6分）

A.　　　　B.　　　　C.

D.　　　　E.　　　　F.　　　　G.

1. ＿＿＿＿＿　　2. ＿＿＿＿＿　　3. ＿＿＿＿＿

4. ＿＿＿＿＿　　5. ＿＿＿＿＿　　6. ＿＿＿＿＿

II、Listen to the dialogue and choose the best answer to the question you hear.（根據你所聽到的對話和問題，選出最恰當的答案。）（10分）

（　）7. (A)For 11 hours.　(B)For 9 hours.　(C)For 10 hours.　(D)For 8 hours.

（　）8. (A)For 6 weeks.　(B)For 5 weeks.　(C)For 4 weeks.　(D)For 3 weeks.

（　）9. (A)He's taking off his shoes.　　(B)He's managing.
　　　　(C)He's catching the plane.　　(D)He's packing.

（　）10. (A)20 years old.　(B)22 years old.　(C)29 years old.　(D)30 years old.

（　）11. (A)At home.　　　　　　　　(B)At her friend's home.
　　　　(C)At his friend's home.　　(D)At a shop.

（　）12. (A)In a hotel.　　　　　(B)In a supermarket.
　　　　(C)In a restaurant.　　(D)At a cinema.

( ) 13. (A)Tuesday.　　(B)Sunday.　　(C)Monday.　　(D)Saturday.

( ) 14. (A)45 minutes.　(B)50 minutes.　(C)40 minutes.　(D)55 minutes.

( ) 15. (A)Yes, she can.　(B)Yes, she can't.　(C)No, she can.　(D)No, she can't.

( ) 16. (A)12.00 noon.　(B)12.15 p.m.　(C)11.45 a.m.　(D)12.30 p.m.

Ⅲ、Listen to the passage and decide whether the following statements are True (T) or False (F). （判斷下列句子是否符合你所聽到的短文內容，符合的用 T 表示，不符合的用 F 表示。）（7分）

( ) 17. People in China do not use spoons.

( ) 18. Some people have trouble using chopsticks.

( ) 19. People in the UK do not usually eat chicken's feet or smelly tofu.

( ) 20. In Japan, people help themselves from plates of food in the middle of the table.

( ) 21. Most people in the UK use chopsticks.

( ) 22. In the UK, the cook cuts all the food into small pieces.

( ) 23. In the UK, people help themselves to the food.

Ⅳ、Listen to the dialogue and fill in the blanks. （根據你聽到的對話，完成下列內容，每空格限填一詞。）（7分）

What has Mary done?

● She has tried to get her mother to have some __24__ and 25

● She has asked her mother to have some __26__ soup

● She has asked her mother to drink some __27__ juice

What hasn't Mary's mother done?

● She hasn't eaten anything since __28__

● She hasn't __29__ well for __30__ nights

24. _____　　25. _____　　26. _____　　27. _____

28. _____　　29. _____　　30. _____

夏朵英文

國中全新英語聽力測驗試題

Unit 5

Ⅰ、Listen and choose the right picture.（根據你所聽到的內容，選出相應的圖片。）（6分）

A.　　　　　　B.　　　　　　C.

D.　　　　　　E.　　　　　　F.　　　　　　G.

1. ＿＿＿＿＿＿　　2. ＿＿＿＿＿＿　　3. ＿＿＿＿＿＿
4. ＿＿＿＿＿＿　　5. ＿＿＿＿＿＿　　6. ＿＿＿＿＿＿

Ⅱ、Listen to the dialogue and choose the best answer to the question you hear.（根據你所聽到的對話和問題，選出最恰當的答案。）（10分）

(　) 7. (A)On foot. 　　(B)By bus. 　　(C)By bike. 　　(D)By taxi.

(　) 8. (A)At 2.00. 　　(B)At 2.05. 　　(C)At 2.10. 　　(D)At 2.20.

(　) 9. (A)100 dollars. 　(B)50 dollars. 　(C)25 dollars. 　(D)20 dollars.

(　) 10. (A)Some students. (B)One student. (C)Some teachers. (D)One teacher.

(　) 11. (A)Terrible. 　　(B)Just so-so. 　(C)Well done. 　　(D)The best.

(　) 12. (A)She doesn't like the film. 　　(B)She has seen the film.
　　　　　(C)She'd like to stay at home. 　(D)She likes watching TV.

(　) 13. (A)In Shanghai Library. 　　(B)On Huaihai Road.
　　　　　(C)On the bus. 　　　　　　(D)On the underground.

( ) 14. (A)In 1998. (B)In 1999. (C)In 2000. (D)In 2001.

( ) 15. (A)The man. (B)The woman.

(C)Both of them. (D)Neither of them.

( ) 16. (A)Because he worked hard at English.

(B)Because he is not interested in English.

(C)Because he didn't pass the Chinese test.

(D)Because he failed in the English test.

Ⅲ、Listen to the passage and decide whether the following statements are True (T) or False (F). （判斷下列句子是否符合你所聽到的短文內容，符合的用 T 表示，不符合的用 F 表示。）（7分）

( ) 17. Jean Champollion learned about twenty languages in his life.

( ) 18. Jean became very interested in ancient Egypt when he was young.

( ) 19. Jean started to study the Rosetta Stone in 1921.

( ) 20. Some scientists found the Rosetta Stone under the sand when Jean was a small boy.

( ) 21. There was a lot of strange writing on the stone.

( ) 22. Ancient Egyptian was a language with letters and words like English.

( ) 23. Jean thought that some of the signs on the Rosetta Stone told about sounds.

Ⅳ、Listen to the dialogue and fill in the blanks. （根據你聽到的對話，完成下列內容，每空格限填一詞。）（7分）

● There are more than __24__ different languages in the world.

● __25__ is the language with the most speakers （more than __26__ speakers）.

● __27__ is the second （more than __28__ speakers）.

● Some languages have a few speakers—about 40 or __29__.

● Some languages __30__ when grandparents pass away.

24. _____ 25. _____ 26. _____ 27. _____

28. _____ 29. _____ 30. _____

夏朵英文
國中全新英語聽力測驗試題
Unit 6

Ⅰ、Listen and choose the right picture.（根據你所聽到的內容，選出相應的圖片。）（6分）

A.　　　　　　B.　　　　　　C.

D.　　　　E.　　　　F.　　　　G.

1. _____　　2. _____　　3. _____
4. _____　　5. _____　　6. _____

Ⅱ、Listen to the dialogue and choose the best answer to the question you hear.（根據你所聽到的對話和問題，選出最恰當的答案。）（10分）

(　　) 7. (A)At 5.45a.m.　(B)At 6.15a.m.　(C)At 6.45a.m.　(D)At 6.55a.m.

(　　) 8. (A)　　　　　　(B)　　　　　　(C)　　　　　　(D)

(　　) 9. (A)Because she was late for the bus.　(B)Because the picnic is terrible.
　　　　　(C)Because the TV play is interesting.　(D)Because it was raining hard.

(　　) 10. (A)Yes, both of them liked it.
　　　　　(B)No, neither of them liked it.
　　　　　(C)His father didn't like it, but his mother did.
　　　　　(D)His mother didn't like it, but his father did.

( ) 11. (A)To have some fish. (B)To have some meat.
　　　 (C)To have some vegetables. (D)To have some chicken.

( ) 12. (A)He has been to the city centre before.
　　　 (B)He is too busy.
　　　 (C)He doesn't like the city center.
　　　 (D)He will not go to the city center.

( ) 13. (A)At home. (B)In the hospital.
　　　 (C)In the library. (D)On the playground.

( ) 14. (A)She has a cold. (B)She has toothache.
　　　 (C)She has a cough. (D)She has a stomachache.

( ) 15. (A)By bus. (B)By train. (C)By plane. (D)By ship.

( ) 16. (A)Teacher and student. (B)Husband and wife.
　　　 (C)Father and daughter. (D)Mother and son.

Ⅲ、Listen to the passage and tell whether the following statements are true or false.（判斷下列句子是否符合你所聽到的短文內容, 符合的用"T"表示，不符合的用"F"表示。）（7分）

( ) 17. Stephen Hawking was born in Oxford and once studied in Cambridge University.

( ) 18. As a university student, Stephen Hawking worked hard and got good marks.

( ) 19. Stephen Hawking first noticed something was wrong with him when he was 23.

( ) 20. Stephen Hawking changed his life attitude after he came out of the hospital.

( ) 21. Later Stephen Hawking married and there were three people in his family.

( ) 22. Stephen Hawking did some scientific researches and now works as a professor at Oxford University.

( ) 23. From the passage, we know that we shouldn't lose hope even in a bad situation.

Ⅳ、Listen to the passage and fill in the blanks.（根據你聽到的短文，完成下列內容，每空格限填一詞。）（7分）

● Marco Daniel wants some information about the __24__ club.

● The members in the club meet every __25__ evening.

- Matches on Sunday morning are just for their __26__ players.
- The meetings begin at __27__, and are about two hours long.
- People like to get home before 10:15 to watch the __28__ program on TV.
- They meet in the Jubilee Hall in Park Lane, behind __29__ Street.
- The hall doesn't have very good heating, so Marco Daniel should take a __30__ to put on afterwards.

24. _____ 25. _____ 26. _____ 27. _____

28. _____ 29. _____ 30. _____

夏朵英文

國中全新英語聽力測驗試題

Unit 7

Ⅰ、Listen and choose the right picture.（根據你所聽到的內容，選出相應的圖片。）（6分）

A.   B.   C.

D.   E.   F.   G.

1. _____   2. _____   3. _____
4. _____   5. _____   6. _____

Ⅱ、Listen to the dialogue and choose the best answer to the question you hear.（根據你所聽到的對話和問題，選出最恰當的答案。）（10分）

( ) 7.　(A)Maths.　　　　(B)Sports.　　　　(C)Music.　　　　(D)Science.

( ) 8.　(A)Tom wants to do it by himself.　　(B)Tom doesn't think it's so hard.
　　　　(C)Tom is very clever.　　　　　　　(D)His mother can't work it out.

( ) 9.　(A)At the school.　　　　　　　　　(B)At the school library.
　　　　(C)On the playground.　　　　　　　(D)At home.

( ) 10.　(A)The man got a new receipt.　　　(B)The man got his radio repaired.
　　　　(C)The man got a new radio.　　　　(D)The man left there without a radio.

( ) 11.　(A)Mike.　　　(B)Mike's mother.　(C)Mike's sister.　(D)Mike's father.

( ) 12. (A)Before class. (B)During the class.
(C)After class. (D)In the classroom.

( ) 13. (A)By bus. (B)By bike. (C)By car. (D)On foot.

( ) 14. (A)Five minutes. (B)Fifteen minutes.
(C)Twenty minutes. (D)Twenty-five minutes.

( ) 15. (A)We don't know from this passage. (B)The girl.
(C)Wang Pen. (D)Li Ming.

( ) 16. (A)She's too busy to go. (B)She's not interested in it.
(C)She hasn't got any tickets. (D)She's ill.

Ⅲ、Listen to the passage and decide whether the following statements are True (T) or False (F). (判斷下列句子內容是否符合你所聽到的短文內容，符合的用 T 表示，不符合的用 F 表示。) (7分)

( ) 17. Kelly always wanted to be an astronaut to work in space one day.

( ) 18. Kelly always thought that she would discover some important things in the future.

( ) 19. One night, Kelly saw a strange, coloured light moving across the sky in the park with her dog.

( ) 20. Kelly thought the light was from a spaceship.

( ) 21. The spaceship landed a few metres in front of Kelly.

( ) 22. Kelly was able to understand what the aliens in the spaceship said.

( ) 23. Kelly's dog went up to the spaceship and never came back again.

Ⅳ、Listen to the dialogue and fill in the blanks. (根據你聽到的對話，完成下列內容，每空格限填一詞。) (7分)

● People will live on the __24__. They will also live in __25__ houses by the year 2100.

● __26__ will cure every illness in the future and people will live __27__ than ever.

● People will have __28__ in space and live on other __29__.

● People will run out of energy sources in the future so people must try to protect the __30__.

24. _____ 25. _____ 26. _____ 27. _____

28. _____ 29. _____ 30. _____

夏朵英文

國中全新英語聽力測驗試題

Unit 8

Ⅰ、Listen and choose the right picture.（根據你所聽到的內容，選出相應的圖片。）（6分）

A.　　　　　　B.　　　　　　C.

D.　　　　　　E.　　　　　　F.　　　　　　G.

1. ＿＿＿＿＿　　2. ＿＿＿＿＿　　3. ＿＿＿＿＿

4. ＿＿＿＿＿　　5. ＿＿＿＿＿　　6. ＿＿＿＿＿

Ⅱ、Listen to the dialogue and choose the best answer to the question you hear.（根據你所聽到的對話和問題，選出最恰當的答案。）（10分）

（　）7. (A)England.　　(B)China.　　(C)America.　　(D)Russia.

（　）8. (A)By bus.　　(B)By bike.　　(C)By car.　　(D)By taxi.

（　）9. (A)Some rice.　　　　　　　(B)Some fish.
　　　　(C)Some meat.　　　　　　(D)Some spicy sausages.

（　）10. (A)Watching TV.　　　　　(B)Cleaning the floor.
　　　　　(C)Reading a book.　　　　(D)Washing the skirt.

（　）11. (A)He went to the zoo.　　　(B)He played basketball.
　　　　　(C)He saw a film last Saturday.　(D)He went to the movies.

( ) 12. (A)By bus.   (B)By underground.
       (C)By bike.   (D)On foot.
( ) 13. (A)In the library.   (B)At the post office.
       (C)At the supermarket.   (D)At the cinema.
( ) 14. (A)5 yuan.   (B)6 yuan.   (C)7 yuan.   (D)8 yuan.
( ) 15. (A)Tuesday.   (B)Wednesday.   (C)Thursday. (D)Friday.
( ) 16. (A)   (B)   (C)   (D)

Ⅲ、Listen to the passage and decide whether the following statements are True (T) or False (F). (判斷下列句子是否符合你所聽到的短文內容，符合的用 T 表示，不符合的用 F 表示。) (7 分)

( ) 17. P2 is the first robot to walk upstairs.

( ) 18. P2 does not look like an astronaut.

( ) 19. Professor Tachi called P2 "humanoid" because it is like a human.

( ) 20. P2 will do some of the work for humans in the next five years.

( ) 21. P2 can think like a human.

( ) 22. The robots will work in all parts of the factory.

( ) 23. It will be a long time before a robot can think like a human according to Professor Tachi.

Ⅳ、Listen to the passage and fill in the blanks. (根據你聽到的短文，完成下列內容，每空格限填一詞。) (7 分)

● David Vetter was born with a strange __24__.

● He became __25__ with 26, water, __27__ and many other things because they were not __28__ enough for him.

● He lived in a __29__ bubble.

● He talked to his parents through the speaker __30__ the bubble.

24. _____   25. _____   26. _____   27. _____
28. _____   29. _____   30. _____

夏朵英文

國中全新英語聽力測驗試題

Unit 9

Ⅰ、Listen and choose the right picture.（根據你所聽到的內容，選出相應的圖片。）（6分）

A.　　　　　　B.　　　　　　C.

D.　　　　　　E.　　　　　　F.　　　　　　G.

1. _____　　2. _____　　3. _____

4. _____　　5. _____　　6. _____

Ⅱ、Listen to the dialogue and choose the best answer to the question you hear.（根據你所聽到的對話和問題，選出最恰當的答案。）（10分）

（　）7. (A)Once a year.　(B)Twice a year.　(C)Three times a year.　(D)Four times a year.

（　）8. (A)Spring.　(B)Summer.　(C)Autumn.　(D)Winter.

（　）9. (A)To the cinema.　(B)To the playground.
　　　　(C)To the park.　(D)To the classroom.

（　）10. (A)A doctor.　(B)A teacher.　(C)Mum.　(D)Sister.

（　）11. (A)At half past four.　(B)At five.
　　　　 (C)At half past five.　(D)At six.

( ) 12. (A)The spring of 2003. (B)The summer of 2003.
(C)The autumn of 2003. (D)The winter of 2003.

( ) 13. (A)Japan. (B)America. (C)Europe. (D)France.

( ) 14. (A)No, he does. (B)Yes, he does. (C)No, he doesn't. (D)Yes, he doesn't.

( ) 15. (A)By bus. (B)By taxi. (C)By underground. (D)On foot.

( ) 16. (A)In the cinema. (B)At the bus stop. (C)At school. (D)At home.

Ⅲ、Listen to the passage and decide whether the following statements are True (T) or False (F). (判斷下列句子是否符合你所聽到的短文內容，符合的用 T 表示，不符合的用 F 表示。)（7分）

( ) 17. The War of the Worlds was a book about spaceships coming from the Earth.

( ) 18. H. G. Wells was the man who put out a radio programme from the book.

( ) 19. In the programme, the actors talked like reporters and the listeners thought it was a real news report.

( ) 20. In the progamme, the actors told the listeners that creatures from other plants would attack the people on Earth.

( ) 21. No one believed what the actors said on the radio.

( ) 22. Orson Welles didn't tell the listeners the truth until 40 minutes later.

( ) 23. It seems that people often play jokes on other people and try to scare them on Halloween.

Ⅳ、Listen to the dialogue and fill in the blanks. (根據你聽到的對話，完成下列內容，每空格限填一詞。)（7分）

● Liu Mei and Wang Gang are talking about the following books: The War of the Worlds, The __24__ Men in the __25__, The Invisible Man and The __26__ Machine.

● Wang Gang says the book is about a scientist who builds a machine and travels to the __27__. He discovers a lot of __28__ things.

● Liu Mei is interested in discovering new __29__. She needs to study for the __30__ exam first.

24. _____   25. _____   26. _____   27. _____

28. _____   29. _____   30. _____

夏朵英文

國中全新英語聽力測驗試題

Unit 10

I、Listen and choose the right picture.（根據你所聽到的內容，選出相應的圖片。）（6分）

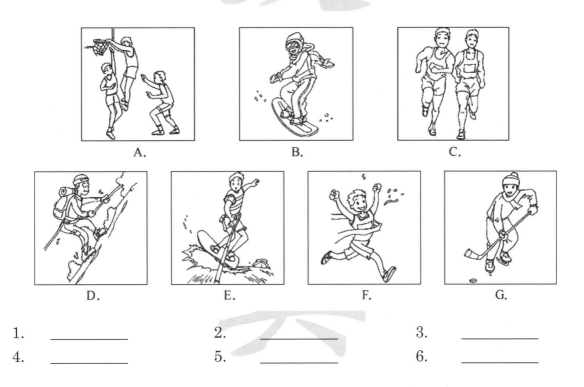

A.　　　　　　B.　　　　　　C.

D.　　　　　E.　　　　　F.　　　　　G.

1. _____　　2. _____　　3. _____
4. _____　　5. _____　　6. _____

II、Listen to the dialogue and choose the best answer to the question you hear.（根據你所聽到的對話和問題，選出最恰當的答案。）（10分）

(　) 7. (A)To watch the snow.　　　　(B)To clean the street.
　　　　(C)To make a snowman.　　　(D)To make a snow ball.

(　) 8. (A)America.　　(B)Britain.　　(C)France.　　(D)Britain.

(　) 9. (A)He went to study in Britain.
　　　　(B)He went to work in Britain.
　　　　(C)He went to visit Britain.
　　　　(D)He went to London and lived with his brother.

(　) 10. (A)In 2001.　　(B)In 2002.　　(C)In 2003.　　(D)In 2004.

( ) 11. (A)At a shop.　　　　　　　　　(B)At home.

　　　(C)At a library.　　　　　　　(D)In a classroom.

( ) 12. (A)At ten past two.　　　　　　(B)At two.

　　　(C)At twenty past two.　　　　(D)At half past two.

( ) 13. (A)Twenty yuan.　　　　　　　(B)Seventeen yuan.

　　　(C)Eighteen yuan.　　　　　　(D)Nineteen yuan.

( ) 14. (A)A doctor.　　　　　　　　　(B)An engineer.

　　　(C)A computer engineer.　　　(D)A teacher.

( ) 15. (A)At 2.00.　　　(B)At 2.15.　　　(C)At 2.30.　　　(D)At 2.45.

( ) 16. (A)Rainy.　　　(B)Cloudy.　　　(C)Snowy.　　　(D)Sunny.

Ⅲ、Listen to the passage and decide whether the following statements are True (T) or False (F).（判斷下列句子是否符合你所聽到的短文內容，符合的用 T 表示，不符合的用 F 表示。）（7 分）

( ) 17. David has more than a thousand stamps.

( ) 18. David puts his sports stamps with other stamps from the same country.

( ) 19. You cannot make new friends when you go fishing, according to Sally.

( ) 20. Sally thinks eating fish is better than catching them.

( ) 21. Simon's model planes sometimes crash.

( ) 22. Simon learns a lot about real planes from mending his model planes.

( ) 23. The three students are talking about their hobbies.

Ⅳ、Listen to the dialogue and fill in the blanks.（根據你聽到的對話，完成下列內容，每空格限填一詞。）（7 分）

Some facts about the match by Manchester United

● ＿24＿ goals took place in the last two minutes.

● First they ＿25＿ and later they ＿26＿.

● About posters

● David has got some ＿27＿ posters of David Beckham.

● Simon has got two posters of Manchester United Football Team from his ＿28＿.

● Sally wants a poster of Celine Dion and she thinks ＿29＿ only think of ＿30＿.

24. _____　　25. _____　　26. _____　　27. _____

28. _____　　29. _____　　30. _____

夏朵英文
國中全新英語聽力測驗試題
Unit 11

I、Listen and choose the right picture.（根據你所聽到的內容，選出相應的圖片。）（6分）

A.　　　　　B.　　　　　C.

D.　　　　　E.　　　　　F.　　　　　G.

1. _____　　　2. _____　　　3. _____

4. _____　　　5. _____　　　6. _____

II、Listen to the dialogue and choose the best answer to the question you hear.（根據你所聽到的對話和問題，選出最恰當的答案。）（10分）

( ) 7. (A)Swimming.　　(B)Running.　　(C)Skating.　　(D)Boating.

( ) 8. (A)Sue.　　(B)Betty.　　(C)Sharon.　　(D)Alice.

( ) 9. (A)History.　　(B)Math.　　(C)English.　　(D)Chinese.

( ) 10. (A)Rainy.　　(B)Sunny.　　(C)Windy.　　(D)Cloudy.

( ) 11. (A)40.　　(B)30.　　(C)20.　　(D)10.

( ) 12. (A)On Monday.　　(B)On Tuesday.　　(C)On Wednesday.　　(D)On Thursday.

( ) 13. (A)By ship.　　(B)By bus.　　(C)By bike.　　(D)On foot.

( ) 14. (A)Go to the cinema.　　　　(B)Go shopping.
　　　　(C)Go to school.　　　　(D)Go to the stadium.

( ) 15. (A)She isn't a good cook. (B)The fish isn't delicious.
(C)He doesn't want to eat more. (D)He wants to eat more fish.

( ) 16. (A)In a library. (B)In a restaurant. (C)In a school. (D)In a shop.

Ⅲ、Listen to the passage and tell whether the following statements are true or false.（判斷下列句子是否符合你所聽到的短文內容，符合的用"T"表示，不符合的用"F"表示。）（7分）

( ) 17. Many people are donating（捐贈） money to a taxi driver because of his honesty.

( ) 18. Mr Gray, the taxi driver, found a bag with 14,580 in the back of his taxi.

( ) 19. People donated money to Mr Gray before they learned of the story on the Internet.

( ) 20. The couple forgot to take the bag with them when they got off.

( ) 21. Mr Gray found the bag in his taxi and returned it to the couple on the same day.

( ) 22. People thanked Mr Gray for his honesty in different ways.

( ) 23. This passage is mainly about how to tell a story on the Internet.

Ⅳ、Listen to the passage and fill in the blanks. （根據你聽到的短文，完成下列內容，每空格限填一詞。）（7分）

● Kate Ross comes from England and she is __24__ years old.

● Kate wants to visit Asia before she goes to __25__.

● She knows a lot about Nepal and now lives in the __26__ of the country.

● The family has a big house and many __27__ and cousins live with them.

● Kate has been taken to many parties on __28__ evenings since she arrived.

● Kate teaches writing, grammar and __29__ at a small school.

● She is not __30__ which countries she will visit.

24. _____ 25. _____ 26. _____ 27. _____
28. _____ 29. _____ 30. _____

夏朵英文

國中全新英語聽力測驗試題

Unit 12

Ⅰ、Listen and choose the right picture. (根據你所聽到的內容,選出相應的圖片。)（6分）

A.   B.   C.

D.   E.   F.   G.

1. _____   2. _____   3. _____

4. _____   5. _____   6. _____

Ⅱ、Listen to the dialogue and choose the best answer to the question you hear. (根據你所聽到的對話和問題,選出最恰當的答案。)（10分）

（　）7. (A)He can carry the box.   (B)The box is very heavy.
           (C)Tom needs some help.   (D)He can't carry the box.

（　）8. (A)She studied English and then watched TV.
           (B)She studied English instead of watching TV.
           (C)She watched TV after she studied English.
           (D)She studied English by watching TV.

（　）9. (A)2.30.   (B)2.40.   (C)2.45.   (D)3.00.

（　）10. (A)The man.   (B)The woman.
            (C)Both of them.   (D)Neither of them.

（　）11. (A)To have a talk.   (B)To have an English lesson.
            (C)To attend a lecture.   (D)To play football.

(   ) 12. (A)To buy a dictionary.　　　　(B)To look up the word in the dictionary.
　　　　(C)To borrow a dictionary.　　　(D)To ask the teacher for help.

(   ) 13. (A)To her office.　　　　　　　(B)To school.
　　　　(C)To the market.　　　　　　(D)To stay for supper.

(   ) 14. (A)40,000.　　　(B)30,000.　　　(C)20,000.　　　(D)10,000.

(   ) 15. (A)Some chicken.　　　　　　　(B)Some chocolate.
　　　　(C)Some fruit.　　　　　　　(D)Some vegetables.

(   ) 16. (A)The doctor.　　　　　　　(B)The headmaster.
　　　　(C)The teacher.　　　　　　(D)The student.

Ⅲ、**Listen to the passage and decide whether the following statements are True (T) or False (F).**（判斷下列句子是否符合你所聽到的短文內容，符合的用 T 表示，不符合的用 F 表示。）（7分）

(   ) 17. San Francisco is a cold, dark place.

(   ) 18. According to the passage, it is a long way to walk to the top of the hill if you want to look down on San Francisco Bay.

(   ) 19. Only sports-lovers or food-lovers should visit San Francisco.

(   ) 20. Golden Gate Park is near Golden Gate Bridge.

(   ) 21. You can find a Japanese Tea Garden in the Golden Gate Park.

(   ) 22. In Chinatown you can only get hot Sichuan food.

(   ) 23. San Francisco's Chinatown is bigger than London's.

Ⅳ、**Listen to the passage and fill in the blanks.**（根據你聽到的短文，完成下列內容，每空格限填一詞。）（7分）

About Bangkok — the capital of Thailand

● Streets in Bangkok are __24__
　People must leave __25__ if they go to work in the morning

● Tuk-tuks are like little __26__ with __27__ wheels

● Bangkok is famous for its Floating __28__
　People sell fruit and vegetables from their __29__

● Thai food are usually very __30__

24. _____　25. _____　26. _____　27. _____

28. _____　29. _____　30. _____

夏朵英文

國中全新英語聽力測驗試題

Unit 13

Ⅰ、Listen and choose the right picture.（根據你所聽到的內容，選出相應的圖片。）（6分）

A.

B.

C.

D.

E.

F.

G.

1. _____	2. _____	3. _____
4. _____	5. _____	6. _____

Ⅱ、Listen to the dialogue and choose the best answer to the question you hear.（根據你所聽到的對話和問題，選出最恰當的答案。）（10分）

( ) 7. (A)A walkman and some English tapes.(B)A dictionary.
(C)Some music tapes. (D)A camera and a dictionary.

( ) 8. (A)Mike.　　(B)Tom.　　(C)David.　　(D)Jane.

( ) 9. (A)Fifty-two.　　(B)Twenty.　　(C)Fifty.　　(D)Thirty.

( ) 10. (A)At a bus stop.　　(B)In the underground.
(C)At the railway station.　　(D)At the airport.

( ) 11. (A)65758053.　　(B)65750853.　　(C)65758035.　　(D)65750835.

( ) 12. (A)By taxi.　　(B)By bike.　　(C)By bus.　　(D)On foot.

( ) 13. (A)Yes, she does.　　　　(B)No, she doesn't.

(C)She likes singing songs.   (D)She likes watching TV.

(   ) 14. (A)9.45.   (B)11.05.   (C)10.15.   (D)10.55.

(   ) 15. (A)Four times a year.   (B)Four times a month.

         (C)Three times a month.   (D)Once every six months.

(   ) 16. (A)Black coffee.   (B)Coffee with sugar and milk.

         (C)Coffee with sugar.   (D)Coffee with milk.

Ⅲ、**Listen to the passage and decide whether the following statements are True (T) or False (F).** (判斷下列句子是否符合你所聽到的短文內容，符合的用 T 表示，不符合的用 F 表示。)（7分）

(   ) 17. Trees cool the cities as well as clean the air.

(   ) 18. Trees can reduce sound pollution and make cities beautiful.

(   ) 19. We sometimes can use certain kinds of trees to make medicine.

(   ) 20. When we grow trees, soil in the ground will be washed away.

(   ) 21. In the last 200 years, about 3/4 of the trees on Earth were destroyed.

(   ) 22. Trees for Earth is an organization for protecting trees all over the world.

(   ) 23. The e-mail address of Trees for Earth is info@treesforearth.com.

Ⅳ、**Listen to the dialogue and fill in the blanks.** (根據你聽到的對話，完成下列內容，每空格限填一詞。)（7分）

- Emma and her friends travelled around China by __24__ and sometimes by __25__.

- Ben and his parents were caught in a sandstorm five years ago in Beijing and it was difficult to breathe and the sand even __26__ people.

- Emma found that there were __27__ sandstorms in Beijing this time because people in Beijing are __28__ more trees.

- Ben told Emma that it was dangerous to drink water from the river because some rivers and lakes were polluted by __29__ or dead animals.

- It would be __30__ for them to drink bottled water.

24. _____   25. _____   26. _____   27. _____

28. _____   29. _____   30. _____

夏朵英文

國中全新英語聽力測驗試題

Unit 14

I、Listen and choose the right picture.（根據你所聽到的內容，選出相應的圖片。）（6分）

A.　　　　　B.　　　　　C.

D.　　　　　E.　　　　　F.　　　　　G.

1. _____　　2. _____　　3. _____

4. _____　　5. _____　　6. _____

II、Listen to the dialogue and choose the best answer to the question you hear.（根據你所聽到的對話和問題，選出最恰當的答案。）（10分）

( ) 7. (A)At 2.00.　　(B)At 2.30.　　(C)At 3.00.　　(D)At 3.30.

( ) 8. (A)In a library.　　　　　　(B)In a CD shop.

　　　 (C)In a theatre.　　　　　　(D)In a restaurant.

( ) 9. (A)By bus.　　(B)By bike.　　(C)On foot.　　(D)By car.

( ) 10. (A)Because he has to look after his sister.

　　　　(B)Because he will visit Mary.

　　　　(C)Because he has visited Alice.

　　　　(D)Because she will visit her.

( ) 11. (A)To have a picnic.　　　　　(B)To take some films.

　　　　(C)To go on a trip.　　　　　(D)To buy some food.

( ) 12. (A)Mum and son.　　　　　　(B)Teacher and student.

　　　　(C)Waiter and customer.　　　(D)Host and guest.

( ) 13. (A)Dentist. (B)Nurse. (C)Teacher. (D)Doctor.
( ) 14. (A)64580023. (B)62580023. (C)64850023. (D)62850023.
( ) 15. (A)Coffee and bread. (B)Beef and pork.
(C)Meat. (D)Nothing.
( ) 16. (A)On the phone. (B)At Jenny's home.
(C)At the computer room. (D)At Tom's home.

Ⅲ、Listen to the passage and decide whether the following statements are True (T) or False (F). (判斷下列句子是否符合你所聽到的短文內容，符合的用 T 表示，不符合的用 F 表示。)（7分）

( ) 17. The speakers asked three questions at the beginning and the answers to these questions are all "No".
( ) 18. Grandmother often tells the speaker some stories about her childhood.
( ) 19. It seems that in the city people lived in a cleaner environment many years ago.
( ) 20. The speaker told us that people are doing something bad to the city now.
( ) 21. The speaker thought that the Earth is in trouble.
( ) 22. The speaker seemed to be a member of an organization which helps protect the environment.
( ) 23. The speaker suggested we reuse plastic bags for shopping.

Ⅳ、Listen to the dialogue and fill in the blanks. (根據你聽到的對話，完成下列內容，每空格限填一詞。)（7分）

QUESTIONNAIRE: How do you feel about these 24?
Your choices:
Anot worried at all
Ba __25__ worried
Cvery worried
Question 1: People throwing __26__ in parks, streets and __27__ places.
Your answer: ☐
Question 2: People making a lot of __28__.
Your answer: ☐
Question 3: People __29__ the water and the air.
Your answer: ☐
Question 4: A lot of __30__ on the road.
Your answer: ☐

24. _____ 25. _____ 26. _____ 27. _____
28. _____ 29. _____ 30. _____

夏朵英文

Unit 15

I、Listen and choose the right picture.（根據你所聽到的內容，選出相應的圖片。）（6分）

A.   B.   C.

D.   E.   F.   G.

1. _____ 2. _____ 3. _____
4. _____ 5. _____ 6. _____

II、Listen to the dialogue and choose the best answer to the question you hear.（根據你所聽到的對話和問題，選出最恰當的答案。）（10分）

(　) 7. (A)7.45.   (B)8.20.   (C)8.15.   (D)8.25.

(　) 8. (A)56940213.   (B)56942310.   (C)56639304.   (D)56693304.

(　) 9. (A)At the reception desk.   (B)In Room 5018.
       (C)In a restaurant.   (D)In a bookshop.

(　) 10. (A)By train.   (B)By bus.   (C)By underground. (D)By taxi.

(　) 11. (A)Go to the cinema.   (B)Have a big meal.
       (C)Stay at home.   (D)Go to the airport.

(　) 12. (A)At a restaurant.   (B)In a hotel.
       (C)In a supermarket.   (D)At the cinema.

(　) 13. (A)A dentist.   (B)A doctor.   (C)A teacher.   (D)A trainer.

(   ) 14. (A)12 years old.   (B)14 years old.   (C)15 years old.   (D)16 years old.

(   ) 15. (A)Friendlier.   (B)Not friendly.

          (C)Not as friendly as hers.   (D)As friendly as hers.

(   ) 16. (A)He got up late this morning.

          (B)He hurried off to catch a plane.

          (C)He was afraid that he would be late for the train.

          (D)He hurried off to catch a train.

Ⅲ、Listen to the passage and decide whether the following statements are True (T) or False (F). （判斷下列句子是否符合你所聽到的短文內容，符合的用 T 表示，不符合的用 F 表示。）（7 分）

(   ) 17. According to the passage, the listeners might be the people in the city.

(   ) 18. In this country, if you are under 18 years of age, you may not buy wine, but your friend can buy it for you.

(   ) 19. The speaker told the listeners not to make unnecessary noise at night. But they can in the day time.

(   ) 20. It's important for the listeners to cross the streets by using the pedestrian crossings in England.

(   ) 21. You may buy cigarettes if you are above 16 years of age.

(   ) 22. It is against the law to put the litter in your pocket and take it home.

(   ) 23. A policeman probably makes the speech.

Ⅳ、Listen to the dialogue and fill in the blanks. （根據你聽到的對話，完成下列內容，每空格限填一詞。）（7 分）

Some facts about blind and deaf people

For blind people

●   good __24__ skills are useful for them

●   they __25__ hear better than other people

●   they use their hearing __26__ than people with 27

For deaf people

●   they do things more __28__ than blind people

●   they never get the __29__ to hear the language

●   they use __30__ language to communicate

24. _____   25. _____   26. _____   27. _____

28. _____   29. _____   30. _____

夏朵英文

國中全新英語聽力測驗試題

Unit 16

Ⅰ、Listen and choose the right picture.（根據你所聽到的內容，選出相應的圖片。）（6分）

A. B. C.

D. E. F. G.

1. _____   2. _____   3. _____
4. _____   5. _____   6. _____

Ⅱ、Listen to the dialogue and choose the best answer to the question you hear.（根據你所聽到的對話和問題，選出最恰當的答案。）（10分）

（　）7. (A)Once a year.　　　　　　(B)Twice a month.
　　　　 (C)Twice a year.　　　　　(D)Twice a half year.

（　）8. (A)200.　　(B)300.　　(C)400.　　(D)600.

（　）9. (A)There is not any water.　　(B)He is not so good at swimming.
　　　　 (C)He should watch out before diving.　(D)All of the answers are right.

（　）10. (A)One.　　(B)Two.　　(C)Three.　　(D)Four.

（　）11. (A)Because sunhats are getting cheaper and cheaper.
　　　　　(B)Because he is not able to pay for it.
　　　　　(C)Because his mother is not with him.
　　　　　(D)Because his mother doesn't like the color.

( ) 12. (A)Because he lost his watch. (B)Because his watch is too fast.
(C)Because his watch is too slow. (D)Because his watch doesn't work.

( ) 13. (A)Yes, she did. (B)Yes, she will. (C)No, she didn't. (D)No, she won't.

( ) 14. (A)To the hospital. (B)To his home.
(C)To the school clinic. (D)To the school gate.

( ) 15. (A)Not bad. (B)Well. (C)Beautifully. (D)Wonderful.

( ) 16. (A)9.30. (B)8.30. (C)10.00. (D)10.30.

Ⅲ、Listen to the passage and decide whether the following statements are True (T) or False (F).（判斷下列句子是否符合你所聽到的短文內容，符合的用 T 表示，不符合的用 F 表示。）(7 分)

( ) 17. Our brains can hold a picture for one-tenth of a second.

( ) 18. If we want to form moving pictures in our minds, there needs to be at least twenty pictures a second.

( ) 19. We can make moving pictures on the notebook by ourselves according to the speaker.

( ) 20. Analogue televisions have sound and pictures in numbers.

( ) 21. In fact, an analogue television changes pictures many times each second to make moving pictures.

( ) 22. A digital television doesn't change pictures as often as an analogue television.

( ) 23. According to the speaker, the picture and sound quality of an analogue television is much better.

Ⅳ、Listen to the passage and fill in the blanks.（根據你聽到的短文，完成下列內容，每空格限填一詞。）(7 分)

Using different electricity appliances

Rice cookers

- Keep the __24__ of the pot dry
- Not leave the pot on when it is 25

Washing machines

- Do not put your __26__ in a washing machine when it is on.
- Unplug it when you are not __27__ it.

Microwaves

- Do not turn it on when it is empty, because it might start a __28__.

- Stand 3 to __29__ feet away from the microwave when it is on, just to be on the safe side.

- Before you use any glass or plastic containers in a microwave, make sure they are "microwave safe".

- Do not use __30__ containers in the microwave.

24. _____   25. _____   26. _____   27. _____

28. _____   29. _____   30. _____

夏朵英文

國中全新英語聽力測驗試題

Unit 17

I、Listen and choose the right picture.（根據你所聽到的內容，選出相應的圖片。）（6分）

A.　　　　　　　B.　　　　　　　C.

D.　　　　　　E.　　　　　　F.　　　　　　G.

| 1. _____ | 2. _____ | 3. _____ |
| 4. _____ | 5. _____ | 6. _____ |

II、Listen to the dialogue and choose the best answer to the question you hear.（根據你所聽到的對話和問題，選出最恰當的答案。）（10分）

(　) 7. (A)The pair of black goggles.　　(B)Neither.
　　　　(C)The pair of brown goggles.　　(D)Either.

(　) 8. (A)Because he had gone to bed too late the night before.
　　　　(B)Because he felt ill.
　　　　(C)Because he had little time.
　　　　(D)Because he had a stomachache.

(　) 9. (A)By bike.　　(B)By subway.　　(C)By taxi.　　(D)By bus.

(　) 10. (A)In the street.　　　　(B)In a fruit shop.
　　　　(C)In a flower shop.　　(D)At a restaurant.

(　) 11. (A)She stayed at home.　　(B)She went shopping.
　　　　(C)She went fishing.　　　(D)She watched a match.

( ) 12. (A)At Mike's home. (B)At Rita's home. (C)On the desk. (D)At the school.
( ) 13. (A)30 years old. (B)35 years old. (C)20 years old. (D)55 years old.
( ) 14. (A)12 problems. (B)8 problems. (C)10 problems (D)2 problems.
( ) 15. (A)His Chinese homework. (B)His English homework.
(C)His maths homework. (D)None.
( ) 16. (A)He watched TV.
(B)He learned English by watching TV.
(C)He learned English and then watched TV.
(D)He learned English.

Ⅲ、Listen to the passage and decide whether the following statements are True (T) or False (F). （判斷下列句子是否符合你所聽到的短文內容，符合的用 T 表示，不符合的用 F 表示。）（7分）

( ) 17. Drinking water can be easily polluted and even a litre of oil can pollute 11,250,000 litres of drinking water.
( ) 18. 13,500 litres of water equals to the amount that you drink 56 glasses of water every day for a year.
( ) 19. 65 soft drink cans can hold about 22.5 litres of water.
( ) 20. According to the speaker, 135 litres of water is enough to wash a whole car.
( ) 21. It seems that the water we use to flush toilets each time is of about 80 litres.
( ) 22. It saves water if you take a shower rather than a bath.
( ) 23. The passage tells us some facts about using water.

Ⅳ、Listen to the passage and fill in the blanks. （根據你聽到的短文，完成下列內容，每空格限填一詞。）（7分）

Ways to keep water clean:

● Pick up litter like 24, __25__ bags and cigarette ends before rainwater washes it over.

● Don't throw 26, __27__ or litter down your sink or toilet.

● Pick up your dog's __28__.

● Take household 29, waste oil to the specific sections of official landfills.

● Do not throw litter on nearby __30__.

24. _____ 25. _____ 26. _____ 27. _____

28. _____ 29. _____ 30. _____

夏朵英文

國中全新英語聽力測驗原文及參考答案

Unit 1

I、Listen and choose the right picture.（根據你所聽到的內容，選出相應的圖片。）（6分）

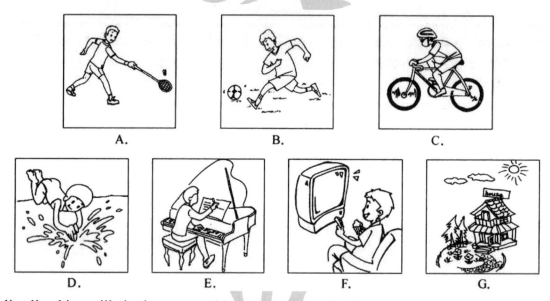

A.　　　　　B.　　　　　C.

D.　　　E.　　　F.　　　G.

1.　Alice lived in a villa in the countryside with her large family.
　　(Alice 和她的大家庭住在鄉村的別墅。)
　　答案：(G)

2.　Simon often practises cycling in the stadium after class.
　　(Simon 課後常常在體育場練習騎腳踏車。)
　　答案：(C)

3.　Would you like to play badminton with me tomorrow?（你明天可以跟我去打羽毛球嗎？）
　　答案：(A)

4.　I have a piano lesson from eight to nine this evening. I can't go to the cinema with you.
　　(今天晚上八點到九點我有鋼琴課。我不能跟你去看電影。)
　　答案：(E)

5.　Judy is a diver. She goes to the swimming pool for training every day.
　　(Judy 是潛水員。她每天去游泳池接受訓練。)
　　答案：(D)

6.　How about watching TV now? I know there's a new play on tonight.
　　現在看電視如何？我知道今天晚上有一齣新的戲劇。
　　答案：(F)

7. W: There are three people in my family. What about yours, John?

    （W: 我家有三個人。John，你呢？）

    M: Five, Kate.(M: Kate，有五個人。)

    Question: Whose family is smaller? (問題：誰的家庭比較小？)

    (A)John's family is bigger.(John 的家庭比較大。)

    (B)John's family is smaller. (John 的家庭比較小。)

    (C)Kate's family is bigger(Kate 的家庭比較大。)

    (D)Kate's family is smaller. (Kate 的家庭比較小。)

    答案：(D)

8. M: These mooncakes are very delicious. Please have a taste, Jane.

    (M: 這些月餅非常好吃。請嚐嚐看，Jane。)

    W: No, thanks. I can't eat any more.(W: 不了，謝謝。我吃不下了。)

    Question: Is Jane hungry? (問題：Jane 餓嗎？)

    (A)Yes, I am.(是的，我餓了。)   (B)Yes, she is. (是的，她餓了。)

    (C)No, I'm not. (不，我不。)   (D)No, she isn't. (不，她不餓。)

    答案：(D)

9. W: Are you good at swimming, Tom?(W: Tom, 你擅長游泳嗎？)

    M: Yes, but I like tennis best.(M: 是，但是我最喜歡網球。)

    Question: What is Tom's favourite sport? (問題：Tom 最喜歡的運動是甚麼？)

    (A)Football.(足球)   (B)Swimming.(游泳)   (C)Tennis.(網球)   (D)Table tennis.(桌球)

    答案：(C)

10. W: May I help you, sir? Do you need any fruit?

    (M: 先生，我能為你服務嗎？你需要水果嗎？)

    M: Let me see. Ah, yes! I want two kilograms of bananas.

    (M: 讓我想想。啊，對了！我要兩公斤的香蕉。)

    Question: Where are they now? (問題：他們現在哪裡？)

    (A)They are in a clothes shop.(他們在服裝店。)

    (B)They are at the fruit stall.(他們在水果攤。)

    (C)They are in the cinema.(他們在電影院。)

    (D)They are at the hospital.(他們在醫院。)

    答案：(B)

11. W: Were you in Guangzhou last week?(W: 你上星期在廣州嗎？)

    M: Yes, I was. I went there for a meeting.(M: 是的，我在。我去那兒參加一場會議。)

    Question: Why did the man go to Guangzhou last week?

    (問題：那男人上星期為什麼去廣州？)

(A)He was travelling there.(他去那兒旅行。)

(B)He had a meeting there.(他在那兒有場會議。)

(C)He went to meet the woman there.(他去那兒和一個女人見面。)

(D)He visited some relatives there.(他去那兒拜訪一些親戚。)

答案：(B)

12. W: I have got two tickets for the football match, Danny. Let's go together, shall we?

    (W: Danny，我有兩張足球票。我們一起去看，好嗎？)

    M: Thank you, I'd love to. When?(M: 謝謝，我很樂意。甚麼時候呢？)

    W: On Sunday evening.(W: 星期天晚上。)

    M: Oh! I am afraid I won't be free at that time.(M: 喔！我那時候恐怕沒空。)

    W: What a pity!(W: 真可惜！)

    Question: Will Danny watch the football match? (問題：Danny 會去看足球賽嗎？)

    (A)Yes, he will.(是的，他會去。)   (B)No, he won't.(不，他不去。)

    (C)Yes, he did.(是的，他去了。)   (D)No, he didn't.(不，他沒去。)

    答案：(B)

13. W: I left my raincoat in the classroom. I will go back to get it. Wait, Tom!

    (W: 我把雨衣留在教室了。我要去把它拿回來。Tom，等等我！)

    M: No, you needn't. The weather report says it will clear up soon.

    (M: 你不需要去。氣象報告說馬上就放晴了。)

    Question: What did Tom advise the girl to do? (問題：Tom 建議那女孩做甚麼？)

    (A)He advised her to take her raincoat with her.(他建議她去拿雨衣。)

    (B)He advised her to take her umbrella with her.(他建議她去拿雨傘。)

    (C)He advised her not to take her umbrella with her.(他建議她不要去拿雨傘。)

    (D)He advised her not to take her raincoat with her.(他建議她不要去拿雨衣。)

    答案：(D)

14. M: Which is the most serious kind of pollution, noise pollution, water pollution, land pollution

    or air pollution?(M: 哪一種汙染最嚴重，噪音汙染、水汙染、土壤汙染、還是空氣汙染？)

    W: I think air pollution is the most serious kind of pollution.

    (W: 我認為空氣汙染是最嚴重的污染。)

    Question: What is the most serious kind of pollution according to the woman?

    (問題：根據那女人，哪一種是最嚴重的污染。)

    (A)Noise pollution.(噪音汙染。)   (B)Air pollution.(空氣汙染。)

    (C)Water pollution.(水汙染。)   (D)Land pollution.(土壤汙染。)

    答案：(B)

15. W: Where were you between 7 and 10 o'clock last night?

    (W: 昨天晚上七點到十點之間你在哪裡？)

    M: I went to the cinema with my friend, Andrew.(M:我跟朋友 Andrew 去看電影。)

    W: Where did you meet him?(W: 你在哪裡跟他碰面？)

M: He came to my flat.(M: 他來我公寓。)

W: When?(W: 甚麼時候？)

M: At around half past six in the evening.(M: 差不多晚上六點半。)

Question: Where was Andrew at about half past six yesterday evening?

(問題：昨天晚上六點半左右，Andrew 在哪裡？)

(A)At the boy's flat.(在那男孩的公寓。)　　　(B)At the girl's flat.(在那女孩的公寓。)

(C)At the cinema.(在電影院。)　　　(D)At his own home.(在他家。)

答案：(A)

16. M: Tomorrow is Saturday. We needn't work in the office. I want to see a film. Will you go with me?(M: 明天是星期六。我們不需要在辦公室上班。我想去看電影。你要跟我去嗎？)

W: My brother has asked me to play tennis, but I want to breathe some fresh air.

(W: 我哥哥找我去打網球，但是我想去呼吸新鮮空氣。)

Question: What is the possible relationship between the two speakers?

(問題：這兩個談話者之間可能是甚麼樣的關係？)

(A)Brother and sister.(兄弟姊妹。)　　　(B)Father and daughter.(父女。)

(C)Son and mother.(母子。)　　　(D)Workmates.(同事。)

答案：(D)

Ⅲ、Listen to the letter and decide whether the following statements are True (T) or False (F). （判斷下列句子是否符合你所聽到的信件的內容，符合的用 T 表示，不符合的用 F 表示。）（7分）

Dear Kelly,

　　Do you like this photo of me with my school friends? I am in glasses. Can you see me? On the right is Sally. She is British. She is my best friend at school. She is always happy to help everyone. On the left is Alice. I play table tennis with her every afternoon.

　　The boys stand behind us. Danny wears glasses too. He is a painter. His paintings are very beautiful. He is also a basketball player on the school team. Our school team often wins the Middle School Championship in the city. Peter is a very good swimmer. He practises every morning and night. He wants to be one of the best swimmers in the world. He is the boy next to Jack. Jack is the tallest boy in the class. He is good at tennis. His favourite tennis player is Roger Federer. Bill is the boy on the right. He is not very good at sports, but he is very friendly to everyone around him. We all like him a lot.

　　Please write to me soon and tell me about your friends.

Love,

Kitty

親愛的 Kelly，

　　妳喜歡這張我和學校朋友的合照嗎？我戴眼鏡。你看到我了嗎？右邊的是 Sally。她是英國人。她是我在學校最好的朋友。她總是很樂意幫助他人。左邊的是 Alice。我跟她每天下午一起打桌球。

　　男生們站在我們的後面。Danny 也戴眼鏡。他是一位畫家。他的畫作非常漂亮。他也是校隊的籃球選手。我們的校隊經常贏得本市的中學冠軍。Peter 是一位很棒的游泳選手。他每天早晚練習。他想成為世界上最棒的游泳選手之一。他是站在 Jack 隔壁的那個男生。Jack 是班上最高的男生。他擅長網球。他最喜歡的網球選手是 Roger Federer。Bill 是在右邊的那個男生。他不擅長運動，但是他對他身邊的每個人都很友善。我們都很喜歡他。

　　請快回信，跟我聊聊你的朋友。

愛你的，Kitty

17. Kitty receives a letter from Kelly. (Kitty 收到一封 Kelly 寫來的信。)

　　答案：(F 錯)

18. Sally, who stands on the right of Kitty, is from the UK.(站在 Kitty 右邊的 Sally 是英國人。)

　　答案： (T 對)

19. Kelly usually plays table tennis with Alice at school. (Kelly 常常在學校和 Alice 一起打桌球。)

　　答案：(F 錯)

20. Danny can draw very well. (Danny 畫圖畫得非常好。)

　　答案： (T 對)

21. Peter practises playing tennis every day.(Peter 每天練習打網球。)

　　答案：(F 錯)

22. Bill is quite good at sports. (Bill 相當擅長於運動。)

　　答案：(F 錯)

23. Kitty wants to know something about Kelly's friends.

　　(Kitty 想知道一些關於 Kelly 的朋友的事。)

　　答案：(T 對)

Ⅳ、**Listen to the passage and fill in the blanks.** (根據你聽到的短文，完成下列內容，每空格限填一詞。)(7分)

　　Jane is my classmate. She is twelve years old and one hundred and sixty centimetres tall. She is an American girl. She is from New York. She has big blue eyes. Her hair is not black. It is brown. Jane speaks English and she can speak a little Chinese, too. Both of her parents are engineers. She has a sister. Her name is Helen. She is twenty-one years old. She is an architect in New York.

　　It is Tuesday. Jane and I are very busy. Jane is carrying a bucket of water to the classroom. The water is heavy. I am washing the blackboard and Jane is cleaning the floor. Soon, the classroom is nice and clean.

　　Jane 是我同學。她十二歲，高一百六十公分。她是一個美國女孩。她從紐約來。她有大大的藍眼睛。她的頭髮不是黑色的，而是棕色的。Jane 說英文，她也會說一點中文。她的父母都是工程師。她有一個姊姊。她的名字是 Helen。她二十一歲。她是紐約的建築師。

今天星期二。Jane 和我非常忙。Jane 要搬一桶水去教室。水非常重。我在清洗黑板。Jane 在清掃地板。教室很快的就會很乾淨。

- Jane is __24__ years old. (Jane＿＿歲。)
- Jane is __25__ centimetres tall. (Jane 高＿＿公分。)
- Jane has __26__ hair. (Jane 有＿＿的頭髮。)
- Jane speaks English and she can speak a little __27__. (Jane 說英文，她會說一點＿＿。)
- Jane's parents work as __28__. (Jane 的父母擔任＿＿。)
- Jane's sister, Helen is an __29__. (Jane 的姊姊 Helen 是一位＿＿。)
- Jane is __30__ the floor in the classroom. (Jane 在＿＿教室的地板。)

24. 答案：12/twelve (十二)
25. 答案：160/one hundred and sixty (一百六十)
26. 答案：brown (棕色)
27. 答案：Chinese (中文)
28. 答案：engineers (工程師)
29. 答案：architect (建築師)
30. 答案：cleaning (清理/清掃)

夏朵英文

國中全新英語聽力測驗原文及參考答案

Unit 2

Ⅰ、Listen and choose the right picture.（根據你所聽到的內容，選出相應的圖片。）（6分）

1. Have you ever watched lion dances? It's quite popular in the Chinatown in Melbourne.
   (你看過舞獅嗎？它在墨爾本的中國城相當受到歡迎。)
   答案：(E)

2. It shines brightly today. Shall we go to the park for a walk?
   (今天天氣晴朗。我們去公園散步好嗎？)
   答案：(B)

3. Don't forget to wash your hands before eating. (吃東西前別忘了洗手。)
   答案：(D)

4. Jimmy, cheers! We haven't met for a long time. (Jimmy，乾杯。我們好久沒見面了。)
   答案：(F)

5. Do you enjoy making snowmen in winter? (冬天的時候你喜歡做雪人嗎？)
   答案：(G)

6. Take a hot shower and you will feel much better. (沖個熱水澡，你就會覺得好一點。)
   答案：(C)

7. W: Why hasn't Linda come? It's nearly 3.30.(W: Linda 為什麼還不來？已經要三點半了。)

   M: I told her to be here at 3.15. She has been late for fifteen minutes.

   (M: 我告訴她三點十五分來這兒。她已經遲到十五分鐘了。)

   Question: What time did the man ask Linda to come? (問題：那男人要 Linda 幾點來？)

   (A)Before 3.15.(三點十五分以前。)　　　　(B)At 3.30.(三點三十分。)

   (C)At 3.15.(三點十五分。)　　　　(D)At 3.50.(三點五十分。)

   答案：(C)

8. W: Hi, Tom, I am afraid I have to get my book back. Can you return it to me?

   (W: Tom，我恐怕得要把我的書拿回來。你明天能還我嗎？)

   M: Oh, sorry! It isn't with me. I left it at the doctor's.

   (M: 喔，對不起。它不在我這裡。我把它放在醫生家了。)

   Question: Whose book do you think it is? (問題：你認為這是誰的書？)

   (A)The girl's.(女孩的。)　　　　(B)The boy's.(男孩的。)

   (C)The doctor's.(醫生的。)　　　　(D)Someone else's.(某個人的。)

   答案：(A)

9. W: Danny, what about your examination?(W: Danny，你考試考得怎樣？)

   M: I achieved B grades in Chinese and physics.(M: 我的中文和物理都拿了 B。)

   W: Not bad! And I'm sure you are good at English and music.

   (W: 還不差啊！我相信你的英文和音樂考得很好。)

   M: Yes, they are my favourite subjects. But I failed in history. I just can't remember all the years and events!(M: 是的，它們是我最喜歡的科目。但是我歷史當掉了。我就是記不得那些年分和事件。)

   W: Poor boy!(W: 可憐的孩子！)

   Question: Which subjects are Danny's favorite? (問題：Danny 最喜歡哪些科目？)

   (A)Chinese and physics.(中文和物理。)　　　　(B)English and music.(英文和音樂。)

   (C)History and music.(歷史和音樂。)　　　　(D)English and history.(英文和歷史。)

   答案：(B)

10. M: Hello, May. We are sure coming to see you next week.

   (M: 哈囉，May。我們下星期一定會來看你。)

   W: I'm glad to hear it. Have you got your plane tickets yet?

   (W: 我很高興聽到你們要來。你買機票了嗎？)

   M: I've already got mine, but Judy hasn't got hers yet. (M: 我已經買了票，但是 Judy 還沒買。)

   W: Why is that?(W: 為什麼？)

   M: She hasn't saved enough money. She is coming to see you by train next week.

(M: 她存的錢不夠。她下星期會搭火車來看你。)

Question: How will Judy go to see her friend next week?

(問題：Judy 下星期要怎麼去看她朋友？)

(A)By plane.(搭飛機。)   (B)By car. (搭車。)

(C)By train. (搭火車。)   (D)By ship. (搭船。)

答案：(C)

11. W: My mother is a manager. She's always busy. What does your mother do, Peter?

    (W: 我母親是一位經理。她總是很忙。Peter，你母親做甚麼？)

M: She's an airhostess for Air France. But when she was a teenager, she hoped to be a pilot. She enjoys her job. (M: 她是法國航空的空中小姐。但是在她還是個青少年的時候，她希望當飛行員。)

Question: What job does Peter's mother do? (問題：Peter 的母親做甚麼工作？)

(A)A manager.(經理。)   (B)A businesswoman.(女企業家。)

(C)A pilot.(飛行員。)   (D)An airhostess.(空中小姐。)

答案：(D)

12. W: I have been to France. I flew back a week ago.(W: 我去了法國。我一個星期前飛回來的。)

M: Did you meet Mary and Joan? They've gone to Paris on business.

    (M: 你見到 Mary 和 Joan 嗎？她們去巴黎出差了。)

W: Yes, I happened to meet them. When I came back, they had already stayed there for two weeks. (W: 是，我碰巧遇見她們。當我回來的時候，她們已經在那兒待了兩個星期。)

M: Are they coming back soon?(M: 她們很快就會回來嗎？)

W: Yes, they said they would return after a week.(W: 是，她們說她們一個星期後回來。)

Question: How long have Mary and Joan been in France?

(問題：Mary 和 Joan 在法國待了多久？)

(A)About two weeks.(大約兩個星期。)   (B)About three weeks.(大約三個星期。)

(C)About four weeks.(大約四個星期。)   (D)About five weeks.(大約五個星期。)

答案：(B)

13. W: I've got two tickets for the film American Pie.(W: 我有兩張「美國派」的電影票。)

M: May I have one?(M: 可以給我一張嗎？)

W: Certainly. I think it's time to leave.(W: 當然可以。我想是時候出發了。)

M: Isn't it still early?(M: 現在不是還早嗎？)

W: Look! It's twenty to two now. It will begin in fifteen minutes.

    (W: 看！現在是一點四十分。它十五分鐘後開演。)

M: You're right, let's hurry.(M: 沒錯，我們得快一點。)

Question: What time will the film begin? (問題：電影幾點開始？)

(A)At 2.55. (兩點五十五分。)   (B)At 1.55. (一點五十五分。)

(C)At 2.40. (兩點四十分。)   (D)At 1.40.(一點四十分。)

答案：(B)

14. M: What can I do for you?(M: 我能為你效勞嗎？)

W: I'd like to have a look at the thick book.(W: 我要看一看那本厚厚的書。)

M: Which one?(M: 哪一本？)

W: The big red one on the shelf.(W: 書架上很大的、紅色的那本。)

M: Here you are. It's expensive. It costs ten pounds.(M: 給你。這本書很貴。要十英鎊。)

Question: Where are they probably talking? (問題：他們可能在哪裡談話？)

(A)In a library.(圖書館。)　　　　　　　　(B)In a book shop.(書店。)

(C)In a reading room. (閱覽室。)　　　　　(D)In the man's home.(那男人的家。)

答案：(B)

15. M: It's too far away to go on foot. I think you should ride a bike.

(M:走路太遠了。我認為你該騎腳踏車。)

W: It's convenient to go by bike, but the traffic is often heavy.

(W: 騎腳踏車很方便，但是交通常常很擁擠。)

M: Then what about taking a bus?(M: 那麼搭公車如何？)

W: But waiting for a bus takes a lot of time. I'd like to take an underground.

(W: 但是等公車要花好久的時間。我想搭地鐵。)

M: That's good.(M: 那很好。)

Question: How would the woman go?(問題：那女人怎麼去？)

(A)By bus.(搭公車。)　　　　　　　　(B)By bike.(騎腳踏車。)

(C)By underground. (搭地鐵。)　　　　　(D)By train.(搭火車。)

答案：(C)

16. M: Can you spell the word "government"?(M: 你能拼出「government」這個單字嗎？)

W: Yes, g-o-v-e-r-m-e-n-t.(W: 可以，g-o-v-e-r-m-e-n-t。)

M: No, you are wrong. You miss an "n".(M: 不，你錯了。你少了一個「n」。)

W: Oh, I see.(W: 喔，我知道了。)

Question: Could the boy spell the word "government"?

(那男孩能拼出「government」這個單字嗎？)

(A)No, he can't.(不，他不能。)

(B)Yes, he can.(是，他可以。)

(C)No, he couldn't. (不，他不可能。)

(D)Yes, he could. (是的，他可能。)

答案：(D)

Ⅲ、Listen to the passage and decide whether the following statements are True (T) or False (F). (判斷下列句子是否符合你所聽到的短文內容，符合的用 T 表示，不符合的用 F 表示。)（7分）

25 Walu Street, Aranda
Canberra ACT 2600
Australia
30 November

Dear Angela,

Thanks for your letter. Now I want to tell you about the four seasons in Canberra.

Spring in Canberra lasts for three months, from September to November. I love the spring here. The trees in the street have lots of small white flowers and the weather is nice. At the beginning of spring, it is cool and sometimes rains. At the end of spring, the weather is warm.

It is often dry and very hot in the middle of summer. Sometimes we have four or five days at 45°C! Our summer holiday starts at the beginning of December and ends at the beginning of February. I go swimming every day. We usually go to the sea for a week in January. It is windy there and the sea is very cool.

In autumn, the trees are all orange and brown. Our autumn is March, April and May.

In winter, it snows in some places. We go skiing in the Snowy Mountains every winter in June, July or August. Sometimes it is rainy but it is usually very cold. Often the sky is very blue, and you never see any clouds. It is my favourite season. What is your favourite season?

Write soon.

Love,
Judy

Walu 街 25 號 Aranda
Canberra 坎培拉 ACT2600
澳大利亞
11 月 30 日

親愛的 Angela，

謝謝你的來信。我現在想告訴你有關 Canberra 的四季。

Canberra 的春天從九月到十一月共持續三個月。我很愛這裡的春天。街道上的樹木有好多白色的小花，天氣也很棒。春天剛開始的時候，天氣很冷而且常常下雨。春天快結束的時候，天氣就很溫暖。

夏天的中期通常非常乾熱。我們有時候有四、五天是攝氏四十五度！我們的暑假在十二月初開始，然後在二月初結束。我每天去游泳。一月的時候我們常常去海邊一個星期。那兒有風，海非常清涼。

秋天的時候，樹木都是橘色和棕色的。我們的秋天是三月、四月和五月。

冬天的時候，某些地方會下雪。每到冬天的六、七、八月，我們常去雪山滑雪。有時會下雨，但是天氣非常冷。天空非常的藍，你完全看不到雲。這是我最喜歡的季節。你最喜歡的季節是甚麼呢？

快回信。

愛你的
Judy

17. Angela has got a penfriend in Australia.(Angela 有一個澳洲的筆友。)

答案：(T 對)

18. Spring in Canberra lasts for about four months. (Canberra 的春天大約持續四個月。)

答案：(F 錯)

19. Summer in Canberra usually starts at the beginning of February. (Canberra 的夏天通常在二月初開始。

答案：(F 錯)

20. Judy enjoys going to the sea in summer. (Judy 喜歡在夏天去海邊。)

答案：(T 對)

21. Judy doesn't talk much about autumn in Canberra in her letter. (Judy 在她的信中並沒有談到很多關於 Canberra 秋天的事。)

答案：(T 對)

22. Winter in Canberra is always rainy and cold. (Canberra 的冬天總是下雨而且寒冷。)

答案：(F 錯)

23. Judy's favourite season is spring.(Judy 最喜歡的季節是春天。)

答案：(F 錯)

IV、Listen to the passage and fill in the blanks.（根據你聽到的短文，完成下列內容，每空格限填一詞。）（7 分）

Anita studies at a middle school in Guangzhou. Every day, she wakes up at six o'clock in the morning. She quickly brushes her teeth and washes her face. Then she reads English for half an hour. She has breakfast at seven o'clock. She usually has two pieces of bread and a glass of milk.

Anita 在廣州念中學。她每天早上六點醒來。她很快地刷牙洗臉。然後她念半個小時的英文。她七點吃早餐。她常吃兩片麵包和一杯牛奶。

After breakfast, Anita goes to school. She lives near school and always walks there. She usually gets to school at eight o'clock, and usually has six lessons. Anita loves English very much, and always gets an A。She usually gets a B in her other subjects.

Anita 吃完早餐後去上學。她住得離學校很近，所以總是走路去。她通常在八點到校，然後有六堂課。Anita 非常愛英文，而且一直拿 A。她通常在其他的科目上拿 B。

After school, Anita usually walks home at four o'clock in the afternoon. Her favourite sport is table tennis. She plays table tennis with her classmates at school once a week.

放學後，Anita 通常在下午四點走路回家。她最喜歡的運動是桌球。她每一星期一次和她的同學在學校打桌球。

Anita often has an early dinner. She begins to do her homework at six o'clock and completes it in one or two hours. She usually goes to bed at nine o'clock.

Anita 晚飯常吃得很早。她六點開始寫功課，在一到兩個小時之內寫完。她通常九點睡覺。

- Anita __24__ up at 6 a.m. (Anita 早上六點_____。)
- After doing some washing, she __25__ English for half an hour. (做了一些清洗之後，她___半個小時的英文。)
- At __26__, she has breakfast. (她___點吃早餐。)
- At 8 a.m., she __27__ to school. (她早上八點_____學校。)
- At 4 p.m., she __28__ home. (她下午四點____回家。)
- At __29__, she begins to do her homework. (她_____點開始寫功課。)
- At 9 p.m., she goes to __30__ . (她晚上九點____。)

24. 答案：wakes (清醒。)
25. 答案：reads (閱讀)
26. 答案：7 a.m. (早上七點)
27. 答案：gets (到達)
28. 答案：walks (走路)
29. 答案：6 p.m. (下午六點)
30. 答案：bed (床)

夏朵英文

國中全新英語聽力測驗原文及參考答案

Unit 3

I、Listen and choose the right picture.

A.   B.   C.

D.   E.   F.   G.

1. Please open the window a bit. We need some fresh air inside.
   (請把窗戶打開一點。我們需要一些新鮮空氣在室內。)
   答案：(G)

2. What a funny man! His pet is a ... P-I-G, pig!
   (多有趣的一個人！他的寵物是一隻…ㄓㄨ，豬！)
   答案：(E)

3. It's very cold outside. You ought to put on your overcoat!
   (外面很冷。你應該穿上你的大衣。)
   答案：(A)

4. Swing, swing, swing! High in the sky! Waving and shaking! It's fun! Win, win, win!
   (盪啊，盪啊，盪啊！高高在天空！揮舞著搖晃著！好好玩！勝利，勝利，勝利！)
   答案：(C)

5. Rope and hope! Jumping and shaking! It's your turn! Let's go on!
   (繩子和希望！跳躍著搖晃著！輪到你了！讓我們繼續！)
   答案：(D)

6. Stop doing that! It's dangerous to ride so fast down the mountain!

（不要那樣做！下山騎那麼快很危險！）

答案：(B)

II、Listen to the dialogue and choose the best answer to the question you hear.

7. M: Excuse me, where is the nearest supermarket? (男：不好意思，最近的超市在哪裡？)

W: I'm sorry. I am new here too. (女：抱歉。我對這一帶也不熟。)

M: Could you tell me where the No. 48 bus is? (男：您可以告訴我四十八路巴士在哪裡嗎？)

W: At the end of the street. (女：在這條街底。)

M: Thank you very much. (男：多謝您。)

Question: Where is the nearest supermarket? (問題：最靠近的超市在哪裡？)

(A)At the corner of the street. (街上的轉角處) (B)At the end of the street. (街道底)

(C)At the No. 48 bus stop. (48 路公車站)　　(D)The lady has no idea. (這位女士不知道。)

答案：(D)

8. M: What can I do for you, madam? (男：有什麼我能為您效勞的，夫人？)

W: I want to buy a handbag. (女：我想買個手提包。)

M: Do you like the blue one or the brown one? (男：您喜歡藍色那個或是咖啡色那個？)

W: I like brown better than blue. How much is it?

　　(女：和藍色的比起來我比較喜歡咖啡色的。它多少錢？)

M: 30 dollars, please. (男：三十美金，麻煩您。)

Question: What is the woman going to buy? (問題：這位女士要買什麼？)

(A)A blue handbag. (一個藍色手提包)　　　　(B)A brown handbag. (一個咖啡色手提包)

(C)13 dollars. (13 元)　　　　　　　　　(D)30 dollars. (30 元)

答案：(B)

9. M: Linda, show me your school report, please. (男：琳達，請給我看妳的學校報告。)

W: Here you are, Daddy. (女：在這裡，爸。)

M: You got good marks for English and chemistry, but you didn't do well enough in maths.

　　(男：妳在英文和化學成績很好，但是妳在數學上表現不夠好。)

W: I'm sorry, Daddy. I'll work harder next time. (女：抱歉，爸。我下次會更用功。)

Question: What subject is Linda poor in? (問題：琳達弱的科目是什麼？)

(A)Physics. (物理)　　(B)English. (英文)　　(C)Maths. (數學)　　(D)Chemistry. (化學)

答案：(C)

10. W: Excuse me, where is the No.49 bus stop? (女：不好意思，四十九路巴士的站在哪裡？)

M: It's just on the other side of the street, near the post office.

　　(男：它就在街道的另一側，靠近郵局。)

W: Thank you. (女：謝謝。)

M: You are welcome. (男：不客氣。)

Question: What is the lady looking for? (問題：這位女士正在找什麼？)

(A)A No. 49 bus. (49 路巴士)　　　　　(B)The bus stop. (巴士站)

(C)The post office. (郵局)　　　　　　(D)A street. (一條街)

答案：(B)

11. W: May I speak to Mr. John Gray? (女：我可以和約翰蓋瑞先生講話嗎？)

　　M: Speaking, who's that calling? (男：我就是，您哪裡找？)

　　W: It's Ellen. Ellen Smith. (女：我是艾倫。艾倫史密斯。)

　　Question: Who are on the phone? (問題：在電話上的是誰？)

　　(A)John and Ellen. (約翰和艾倫)

　　(B)Miss Gray and Mrs. Smith. (蓋瑞小姐和史密斯太太)

　　(C)Mr. Smith and Miss Gray. (史密斯先生和蓋瑞小姐)

　　(D)John and Gray. (約翰和蓋瑞)

　　答案：(A)

12. W: Yesterday I went to see a new film. What about you?

　　　(女：昨天我去看了一場電影。那你呢？)

　　M: I visited the photo show instead of seeing a film.

　　　(男：我參觀了一個攝影展而沒有去看電影。)

　　Question: What did the man do yesterday? (問題：這位男士昨天做了什麼？)

　　(A)He watched TV at home. (他在家看電視。)

　　(B)He went to see a film. (他去看電影。)

　　(C)He visited the photo show. (他參觀了一個攝影展。)

　　(D)He visited the flower show. (他參觀了花展。)

　　答案：(C)

13. M: I can't find my pen. It was here on the desk this morning. Have you seen it, Jim?

　　　(男：我找不到我的筆。它早上在這邊的書桌上。妳有看到它嗎，金？)

　　W: Yes, I wrote a letter with it and then I put it in the desk drawer.

　　　(女：有，我用它寫了一封信然後我把它放在書桌抽屜裡。)

　　Question: What did the girl do with the pen? (問題：這位女孩把那支筆怎麼了？)

　　(A)She gave it to Jim. (她把它給了 Jim。)

　　(B)She put it on the desk. (她把它放在桌子上。)

　　(C)She put it in the desk drawer (她把它放在書桌抽屜裡。)

　　(D)She didn't see it. (她沒看到筆。)

　　答案：(C)

14. W: It's nearly 12 o'clock. I'm hungry. Look, there's a KFC restaurant over there.

　　　(女：將近十二點了。我餓了。你看，在那邊有個肯德基餐廳。)

　　M: But it's expensive, isn't it? (男：但它頗貴，不是嗎？)

　　W: No, it isn't and the chicken there is nice. (女：不會，它不貴而且那邊的雞肉很好。)

　　M: OK. Let's go then. (男：好吧。那我們就去。)

Question: Why are they talking about the KFC fast food?

(問題：他們為什麼在談論肯德基速食？)

(A)Because the restaurant is new. (因為該餐廳是新的。)

(B)Because they enjoy fast food. (因為他們喜歡速食。)

(C)Because the food there is not expensive. (因為那裏的食物不貴。)

(D)Because they are hungry and want to have lunch there.

(因為他們餓了且想要在那邊吃午餐。)

答案：(D)

15. W: Why are you in such a hurry, Mr Black?

(女：你為何如此匆忙，布萊克先生？)

M: I'll leave for Beijing to attend an important meeting. The train will start off in less than two hours. ((男：我將出發去北京出席一個重要的會議。火車將在不到兩小時以內開車。)

W: So you must get everything ready before three o'clock.

(女：所以你必須在三點以前把一切準備好。)

Question: How will Mr Black go to Beijing? (問題：布萊克先生將怎麼去北京？)

(A)By train. (搭火車)　　　　　　　　(B)By plane. (搭飛機)

(C)In about two hours. (在大約兩小時後)　(D)Before three o'clock. (在三點前)

答案：(A)

16. M: Lily, I haven't seen you for nearly a month. Where have you been these days?

(男：莉莉，我快要一個月沒看到妳了。這些日子妳都在哪裡？)

W: I went to Australia with my husband for my holiday.

(女：我和我先生去了澳洲度假。)

M: Did you have a good time there? (男：你們在那邊玩得開心嗎？)

W: Yes. And I'm going to France next summer holiday.

(女：是啊。而且我下個暑假要去法國。)

M: What a coincidence! Me too. (男：多巧啊！我也是。)

Question: Where did Lily go during the holiday? (問題：莉莉在假期中去了哪裡？)

(A)America. (美國)　　(B)Australia. (澳洲)　　(C)France. (法國)　　　(D)Japan. (日本)

答案：(B)

Ⅲ、Listen to the passage and decide whether the following statements are True (T) or False (F).

There will be a lecture at the school lecture hall on Wednesday evening. It's about how to protect eyesight. Nancy has got two tickets, one for herself and the other for her classmate, Henry. Henry is getting quite nearsighted. The lecture is just what he needs. Nancy often forgets things. It's Tuesday today. But she tells Henry to wait for her at the gate of the lecture hall in the evening. There are only five minutes left when Nancy gets there. She shows the tickets. But the ticket-collector won't let them in. The tickets are for tomorrow. The ticket-collector is very kind. There are a couple of tickets for today left. He lets them have the tickets. But it's not the same lecture as tomorrow's. It's about how to train the memory. That's just what Nancy needs.

　　星期三晚上在學校大講堂將會有一場講座。它是關於如何保護視力。南西有兩張票，一張她自己用而另一張給她的同學，亨利。亨利近視得頗重。此講座正好是他需要的。南西常常忘記事情。今天是星期二。但是她告訴亨利晚上在大講堂的大門口等她。當南西到達那裡時只剩下五分鐘了。她把票亮出來。但是收票員不讓他們進去。這票是明天的。收票員很好心。有兩張今天的票剩下。他把票給了他們。但這和明天是不同的講座。這是關於如何訓練記憶力的。正好是南西需要的。

17. There is a lecture on Wednesday evening and another lecture on Thursday evening.
    (星期三晚上有一場講座而星期四晚上有另一場講座。)
    答案：(F 錯)

18. The Wednesday's lecture is about how to protect eyesight.
    (星期三的講座是關於如何保護視力。)
    答案：(T 對)

19. Nancy is sure that Henry will be glad to listen to the lecture.
    (南西確定亨利將會很高興聽這場講座。)
    答案：(T 對)

20. Nancy was late for the lecture. (那場講座南西遲到了。)
    答案：(F 錯)

21. The ticket-collector was a very kind man. (收票員是位很好心的男士。)
    答案：(T 對)

22. Nancy and Henry are not allowed to enter because they are late.
    (南西和亨利不被准許入場因為他們遲到了。)
    答案：(F 錯)

23. It seems that Nancy doesn't remember things very well. (看樣子南西記性不太好。)
    答案：(T 對)

IV、Listen to the passage and fill in the blanks.

　　Yesterday was Eddie's birthday. He got a lot of presents from his friends and family. All the gifts were wrapped in coloured paper. Some of the packages were large, but others were very small. Some were heavy, but others were light. One square package was blue; there was a book in it. Another one was long and narrow; it had an umbrella in the pink paper. Eddie's sister gave him a big, round package. He thought it was a ball, but it wasn't. When he removed the yellow paper that covered it, he saw that it was a globe of the world. After that his brother gave Eddie another gift. It was a big box wrapped in green paper. Eddie opened it and found another box covered with red paper. He removed the paper and saw the third box — this one was blue in colour. Then he saw his brother's gift. He was very happy. It was just what Eddie wanted — a portable computer.

　　昨天是艾迪的生日。他收到很多來自朋友們和家人的禮物。全部的禮物都包著彩色的紙。有一些包裝很大，但其他則很小。有一些很重，但其他的輕。有一個正方形包裹是藍色的；裡面有一本書。另一個又長又窄；它是一把包著粉紅色紙的雨傘。艾迪的姊妹給他一個大的圓形包裹。他以為那是個球，但它不是。當他打開包住它的黃色紙，他看到那是個地球儀。那之後艾迪的兄弟給他另一個禮物。它是個包著綠色紙的大盒子。艾迪打開它而發現了另一個包著紅色紙的盒子。他打開包裝紙而看到第三個盒子——這一個的顏色是藍色的。然後他看到他哥哥的禮物。他很高興。那正是艾迪想要的——一台攜帶型電腦。

- Someone sent Eddie a long and __24.__ package with pink paper outside. It was an __25.__.
  （某人給了艾迪一個又長又窄外面包著粉紅色紙的包裹。它是一把傘。）
- Someone sent Eddie a square package with __26.__ paper outside and a book inside.
  （某人給了艾迪一個正方形外面有藍色紙的包裹裡面是一本書。）
- Eddie also received a globe of the world packed in a big, __27.__ package with yellow paper from his __28.__.
  （艾迪也發現了一個地球儀，包在一個大圓形黃色的包裝紙的包裹裡，來自他姊妹。）
- Eddie received a portable computer packed with __29.__ boxes in green, red and blue paper from his __30.__.
  （艾迪發現了一台攜帶型電腦以三個分別是綠色紅色和藍色的盒子裝著，來自他兄弟。）

24. 答案：narrow (窄)
25. 答案：umbrella (雨傘)
26. 答案：blue (藍色)
27. 答案：round (圓形)
28. 答案：sister (姊妹)
29. 答案：three (三個)
30. 答案：brother (兄弟)

夏朵英文

國中全新英語聽力測驗原文及參考答案

Unit 4

Ⅰ、Listen and choose the right picture.

A. B. C.

D. E. F. G.

1. Mum has put so many decorations on the Christmas tree. It looks very beautiful.
   (媽媽在聖誕樹上放了很多裝飾品。它看起來很漂亮。)
   答案：(D)

2. I'm full. I can't eat up the hamburger. (我吃飽了。我無法吃完這個漢堡。)
   答案：(G)

3. Barbecued meat tastes nice with honey. (烤肉加蜂蜜很好吃。)
   答案：(E)

4. Jackie works as a baker and bakes very nice cakes.
   (傑基的工作是烘焙師並且烘焙出很好的蛋糕。)
   答案：(A)

5. Ben tries to make the flour into a dough. (班試著把麵粉製成麵團。)
   答案：(F)

6. My sister has prepared a big basket of fruits for the picnic.
   (我的姊妹為了野餐準備了一大籃的水果。)
   答案：(C)

7.　W: When does the shop open in the morning? (女：這間商店早上幾點開門？)

　　M: It opens at 9 a.m. (男：它上午九點開。)

　　W: How long is it open? (女：它營業時間多長？)

　　W: It's open till 6 p.m. on weekdays and till 8 p.m. at weekends.

　　　　(男：在週間它營業到下午六點而週末則到晚上八點。)

　　Question: How long is the shop open on Saturday? (問題：此商店星期六營業時間多長？)

　　(A)For 11 hours. (十一個小時)　　　　　　　　(B)For 9 hours. (九個小時)

　　(C)For 10 hours. (十個小時)　　　　　　　　(D)For 8 hours. (八個小時)

　　答案：(A)

8.　W: Dennis, how long have you been in China? (女：丹尼斯，你在中國待多久了？)

　　M: I stayed in Guangzhou for two weeks and in Shanghai for another week. I will go back in

　　　　two weeks. (男：我在廣州停留了兩星期而在上海又一星期。我還有兩星期就要回去了。)

　　Question: How many weeks will Dennis stay in China?

　　(問題：丹尼斯將在中國停留多少星期？)

　　(A)For 6 weeks. (六個星期)　　　　　　　　(B)For 5 weeks. (五個星期)

　　(C)For 4 weeks. (四個星期)　　　　　　　　(D)For 3 weeks. (三個星期)

　　答案：(B)

9.　W: What are you doing, Bob? (女：你在做什麼，包伯？)

　　M: I'm busy packing. The plane will take off in an hour and a half. There is only a little time for

　　　　me to catch it. (男：我忙著收拾行李。班機將在一個半小時後起飛。我只剩一點點時間

　　　　趕飛機。)

　　W: Can I help you? (女：我能幫你嗎？)

　　M: It's all right, thanks. Let me manage it myself. (男：沒關係啦，謝謝。讓我自己搞定。)

　　Question: What is Bob doing now? (問題：包伯現在正在做什麼？)

　　(A)He's taking off his shoes. (他正在脫鞋子。) (B)He's managing. (他正在處理。)

　　(C)He's catching the plane. (他正在趕飛機。)　(D)He's packing. (他在收拾行李。)

　　答案：(D)

10.　W: Long time no see. You seem to be about twenty years old. You were just a kid when I left.

　　　　(女：好久不見。你看起來大約二十歲。當我離開的時候你只是個小孩子。)

　　M: Yes. I was only thirteen years old when you left home nine years ago.

　　　　(男：對。當你九年前離開家時我才十三歲。)

　　Question: How old is the young man? (問題：這位年輕男士幾歲？)

　　(A)20 years old. (二十歲)　　　　　　　　(B)22 years old. (二十二歲)

　　(C)29 years old. (二十九歲)　　　　　　　　(D)30 years old. (三十歲)

　　答案：(B)

11.　W: I'm looking for a pair of brown shoes. (女：我正在找一雙褐色的鞋子。)

M: Sorry, we haven't got brown shoes. But would you like to try on this pair of black shoes? They are very comfortable to wear.

（男：抱歉，我們沒有褐色的鞋子。但妳想要試穿這雙黑色的鞋子嗎？穿起來很舒適。）

Question: Where does this conversation take place? （問題：這段對話在哪裡發生？）

(A)At home. (在家裡)　　　　　　　　(B)At her friend's home. (在她的朋友家)

(C)At his friend's home. (在他的朋友家)　(D)At a shop. (在一間商店)

答案：(D)

12. W: Good evening. My name is Helen. I booked a table by phone two days ago.

（女：晚安。我的名字是海倫。我兩天前以電話預約了一桌。）

M: Please wait a moment. Let me check it for you. Is it the table with ten seats?

（男：請等一下。讓我為您查一查。是一張十位的桌子嗎？）

W: That's right. (女：是的。)

M: OK. This way, please. (男：好。這邊請。)

Question: Where does the conversation probably take place?

（問題：這段對話可能是在哪裡發生？）

(A)In a hotel. (在旅館)　　　　　　(B)In a supermarket. (在超市)

(C)In a restaurant. (在一間餐廳)　　(D)At a cinema. (在電影院)

答案：(C)

13. W: It's very strange that our daughter stayed at home the day before yesterday. She usually goes out for fun on Sundays.

（女：很奇怪，我們的女兒前天待在家裡。星期天她通常會出去找樂子。）

M: She stayed at home in order to wait for a friend. She had a date with the friend of hers. She wanted to ask her for help.

（男：她待在家裡為了等一個朋友。她和她那個朋友有約。她想要找她幫忙。）

Question: What day is it? （問題：今天星期幾？）

(A)Tuesday. (星期二)　(B)Sunday. (星期天)　(C)Monday. (星期一)　(D)Saturday. (星期六)

答案：(A)

14. W: Excuse me, could you please tell me how to get to Shanghai Railway Station?

（女：不好意思，可否請您告訴我怎麼去上海火車站？）

M: Take the second turning on the left. Then walk on to the end of the road. It's fifteen minutes' walk. Take the No.30 bus there. It will take you thirty-five more minutes to get there.

（男：在左邊第二個街口左轉。然後走到那條路的盡頭。這段路要走十五分鐘。在那裡搭三十路巴士。到那裡妳需要再花三十五分鐘。）

Question: How long will it take the woman to get to Shanghai Railway Station?

（問題：去上海火車站將要花這位女士多少時間？）

(A)45 minutes. (四十五分鐘)　　　　(B)50 minutes. (五十分鐘)

(C)40 minutes. (四十分鐘)　　　　　(D)55 minutes. (五十五分鐘)

答案：(B)

15. M: Can you complete the form in five minutes? (男：您可以在五分鐘內填完此表格嗎？)

W: Sorry. I have a phone call to answer now. (女：抱歉。我現在有通電話要接聽。)

Question: The woman can't fill in the form now, can she?

(問題：這位女士現在不能填寫此表格，是嗎？)

(A)Yes, she can. (是的，她能。)　　　　　(B)Yes, she can't. (是的，她不能。)

(C)No, she can. (不，她能。)　　　　　　(D)No, she can't. (不，她不能。)

答案：(D)

16. W: Would you like to attend the lecture given by Dr. Chen?

(女：你會想出席陳博士主講的講座嗎？)

M: I'd love to. When will it begin? (男：我很想去。它幾時開始？)

W: At 1 p.m. I'm afraid we have to hurry. (女：下午一點。我恐怕我們得趕快。)

M: Come on. There is still plenty of time. We have three quarters to get there.

(男：拜託ㄟ。還有很多時間。我們有四十五分鐘時間。)

Question: What time is it now? (問題：現在幾點？)

(A)12.00 noon. (中午十二點)　　　　　(B)12.15 p.m. (下午十二點十五分)

(C)11.45 a.m. (上午十一點四十五分)　　(D)12.30 p.m. (下午十二點半)

答案：(B)

Ⅲ、**Listen to the passage and decide whether the following statements are True (T) or False (F).**

I have had a great time travelling the world, and have learnt a lot about the eating habits of people in different countries.

我在世界各地旅遊很快樂，而且了解到很多不同國家人們的飲食習慣。

In China, for example, people use chopsticks to eat with. They have eaten this way for thousands of years, but I found chopsticks very difficult to use. Chinese cooks usually cut the food into small pieces, and put each dish on a different plate. At dinner, everyone sits at a round table. The hostess puts the dishes of food in the middle of the table, and everyone helps themselves with chopsticks or spoons. In Shanghai, I saw people eat chicken's feet and smelly tofu. I have not seen this kind of food in the UK.

例如，在中國，人們用筷子吃東西。他們以這種方法吃東西幾千年了，但我發現筷子很難用。中國廚師通常把食物切成小塊，然後把各道菜盛放在不同的盤子上。晚餐時，每個人坐在圓桌旁。女主人把一盤盤的菜放在桌子中間，每個人用筷子或湯匙自行取用。在上海，我看到人們吃雞爪和臭豆腐。我在英國沒有看過這類食物。

In Japan, people also use chopsticks, but each person has a separate tray of food. Each tray has several small dishes and bowls of food on it. The people at a table usually do not get food from plates in the middle of the table. The most famous Japanese food is sashimi — raw fish. I found it very delicious.

在日本，人們也用筷子，但是每個人有各別一托盤的食物。每個托盤上有數小碟和數碗食物。同桌的人們通常不會從桌子中間的盤子上取用食物。最有名的日本料理是刺身－生魚。我發現它很好吃。

In the UK, people usually use a knife and fork. For a family dinner, the mother or father will put the food in the middle of the table. Everyone passes the food around. As they pass the food, they take some and put it on their plates. They often eat food like roast beef and potatoes. The father will cut off a large piece of roast beef and put it on each person's plate. They use their knives to cut the food, and their fork to eat it.

在英國，人們通常用刀叉。家族的晚餐，母親或父親會把食物放在桌子中間。每個人傳遞食物一圈。當他們傳遞食物時，他們取用一些然後把它放在自己的盤子上。他們通常吃烤牛肉和馬鈴薯這樣的食物。父親會切下大塊的烤牛肉然後放到每個人的盤子上。他們用他們的刀子切割食物，用他們的叉子來吃。

17. People in China do not use spoons. (在中國的人們不使用湯匙。)

    答案：(F錯)

18. Some people have trouble using chopsticks. (有些人在使用筷子上有困難。)

    答案：(T對)

19. People in the UK do not usually eat chicken's feet or smelly tofu.

    (在英國的人們不常吃雞爪或臭豆腐。)

    答案：(T對)

20. In Japan, people help themselves from plates of food in the middle of the table.

    (在日本，人們從餐桌中間的一盤盤料理自行取用。)

    答案：(F錯)

21. Most people in the UK use chopsticks. (大多數在英國的人使用筷子。)

    答案：(F錯)

22. In the UK, the cook cuts all the food into small pieces. (在英國，廚師把所有食物切成小塊。)

    答案：(F錯)

23. In the UK, people help themselves to the food. (在英國，人們自行取用料理。)

    答案：(F錯)

Ⅳ、Listen to the dialogue and fill in the blanks.

Mr Brown: Marry, are you in a hurry? (布朗先生：瑪莉，妳在趕時間嗎？)

Mary: Yes, I am. Please excuse me, Mr Brown. I must run to the shops to buy some fruit and soya sauce or I shall be late for school.

瑪莉：對，我是。不好意思，布朗先生。我必須跑去店裡買些水果和醬油否則我上學將會遲到。

Mr Brown: Why doesn't your mother do the shopping herself?

布朗先生：為何妳母親不自己採購？

Mary: She is ill. She hasn't eaten any bread or meat since Sunday. She hasn't slept well for two nights.

瑪莉：她生病了。她自從星期天起就沒有吃任何麵包或肉。她兩個晚上都沒有睡好。

Mr Brown: Have you given her some chicken soup? (布朗先生：妳有給她一些雞湯嗎？)

Mary: I've just been to the shop for a chicken, but Mum won't be able to drink the soup. She's very tired all the time. She doesn't want to eat anything. We don't know what to do. We've tried everything.

瑪莉：我剛剛才去店裡買了一隻雞，但我媽無法喝湯。她總是很疲倦。她不想吃任何東西。我們不知道該怎麼辦。我們什麼都試過了。

Mr Brown: Have you asked her to drink some orange juice?

布朗先生：妳有要求她喝一些柳橙汁嗎？

Mary: Yes! I have asked her to drink some orange juice. I guess it is good for her health. I have to go now. See you, Mr Brown.

瑪莉：有！我有要求她喝一些柳橙汁。我猜那對她的健康有益。我現在必須走了。再見，布朗先生。

What has Mary done? (瑪莉做了些什麼？)

● She has tried to get her mother to have some __24__ and __25__
  (她試著讓她母親吃些麵包和肉。)
● She has asked her mother to have some __26__ soup
  (她要求她母親喝些雞湯。)
● She has asked her mother to drink some __27__ juice
  (她要求她母親喝些柳橙汁。)

What hasn't Mary's mother done? (瑪莉的母親沒有做什麼？)

● She hasn't eaten anything since __28__
  (她自從星期天起就沒吃任何東西。)
● She hasn't __29__ well for __30__ nights
  (她兩個晚上沒睡好。)

24. 答案：bread (麵包)
25. 答案：meat (肉)
26. 答案：chicken (雞)
27. 答案：orange (柳橙)
28. 答案：Sunday (星期天)
29. 答案：slept (睡)
30. 答案：two/2 (二)

夏朵英文

國中全新英語聽力測驗原文及參考答案

Unit 5

Ⅰ、Listen and choose the right picture.（根據你所聽到的內容，選出相應的圖片。）（6分）

1. I seldom watch television with my cousins. But yesterday we sat together and watched a very interesting cartoon.

   （我很少跟我表姊弟一起看電視。但是昨天我們坐在一起看了一部很有趣的卡通。）

   答案：(E)

2. Look at Susan! She has fallen asleep but the book is still in her hand.

   （看看 Susan！雖然她睡著了但是書還在她手上。）

   答案：(A)

3. Do people still learn English on the radio today? I know that Teddy does.

   （現在人們依然聽收音機學英文嗎？我知道 Teddy 是這樣的。）

   答案：(B)

4. Have a look at the newspaper. There is an important news report today!

   （看一下報紙。今天有一則非常重要的新聞報導！）

   答案：(C)

5. Some children are making sandcastles on the beach now.

   （一些孩子現在在海邊堆沙堡。）

   答案：(F)

6. Henry laughed happily because he had sent his model plane into the air successfully.
   (Henry 笑得好開心，因為他成功地將他的模型飛機送上天空。)
   答案：(D)

7. W: Tom, can you tell me where the museum is? (W: Tom，你能告訴我博物館在哪裡嗎？)
   M: It's far from here. (M: 那離這裡很遠。)
   W: Can I take a bus there? (W: 我能搭公車去那裡嗎？)
   M: I'm not sure which bus gets there, but you can go there by bike.
      (M: 我不確定哪一班公車會到，但是你可以騎腳踏車去那兒。)
   W: How long will it take me to get there by bike? (W: 騎腳踏車要花多久時間呢？)
   M: About twenty minutes. (M: 差不多二十分鐘。)
   W: Thank you for your advice. (W: 謝謝你的建議。)
   Question: How will the girl probably go to the museum?
   (問題：那女孩大概會怎麼去博物館？)
   (A)On foot. (走路。)   (B)By bus. (搭公車。)
   (C)By bike. (騎腳踏車。)   (D)By taxi. (搭計程車。)
   答案：(C)

8. M: Let's hurry, or we'll be late for the film.
      (M: 我們要快一點，要不然我們看電影就要遲到了。)
   W: What time is it now? (W: 現在幾點？)
   M: It's 2.00 now. There are only twenty minutes left. (M: 現在兩點。只剩下二十分了。)
   W: OK. Shall we take a taxi there? It will take us only five minutes to get there.
      (W: 好。我們搭計程車去那兒好嗎？我們只要花五分鐘就到了。)
   M: But it's expensive. Let's take a bus there. It'll take us about ten minutes.
      (M: 但是那很貴。我們搭公車去吧。大概十分鐘。)
   W: All right. (W: 好。)
   Question: When does the film begin? (問題：電影幾點開始？)
   (A)At 2.00.（兩點。）   (B)At 2.05.（兩點五分。）
   (C)At 2.10.（兩點十分。）   (D)At 2.20.（兩點二十分。）
   答案：(D)

9. M: What can I do for you? (M: 我能為你服務嗎？)
   W: I'm looking for a coat for my son. (W: 我想為我兒子找一件外套。)
   M: We have all kinds and sizes of coats. Which one would you like?
      (M: 我們有各種款式與尺寸的外套。你想要哪一種？)
   W: My son is only a child. I don't want any expensive one.

(W: 我兒子只是個小孩。我不想要太貴的。)

M: I see. This one is 50 dollars, and that one is only 25 dollars.

(M: 我知道了。這件 50 元，那件只要 25 元。)

W: Can I take two with 40 dollars? (W: 我以 40 元買兩件可以嗎？)

Question: How much does the woman want to pay for each coat?

(問題：每一件外套每那女人想花多少錢？)

(A)100 dollars. (100 元)　　　　　　(B)50 dollars. (50 元)

(C)25 dollars. (25 元)　　　　　　(D)20 dollars. (20 元)

答案：(D)

10. W: Where did you go yesterday? (W: 你昨天去哪兒了？)

M: We went to the countryside for a picnic. (M: 我們去鄉下野餐。)

W: How about the outing? (W: 這趟郊遊如何？)

M: Wonderful. The weather was fine and the air was fresh. (M: 非常棒。天氣好，空氣新鮮。)

W: Did your teachers go with you? (W: 你們的老師跟你們一起去嗎？)

M: Yes. We all went there except my deskmate Mike.

(M: 是的。除了我同桌的 Mike 以外我們都去了。)

W: I'm sure you must have had a good time. (W: 我相信你們一定玩得很開心。)

Question: Who didn't go for the picnic? (問題：誰沒去野餐？)

(A)Some students. (一些學生。)　　　(B)One student. (一位學生。)

(C)Some teachers. (一些老師。)　　　(D)One teacher. (一位老師。)

答案：(B)

11. W: Hi, Tom. Why do you look unhappy? (W: 嗨，Tom。你為什麼看起來不開心？)

M: We had a maths exam just now. I didn't do it well. (M: 我們剛剛考完數學。我考得不好。)

W: But how do you know it? (W: 但是你怎麼知道呢？)

M: Some classmates' answers are different from mine. (M: 有些同學的答案和我的不一樣。)

W: Don't worry. Maybe theirs are wrong. (W: 別擔心。或許他們是錯的。)

Question: What does Tom think of his exam? (問題：Tom 覺得他的考試怎麼樣？)

(A)Terrible. (很糟。)　　　　　　　(B)Just so-so. (普通。)

(C)Well done. (很好。)　　　　　　(D)The best. (最好的。)

答案：(A)

12. W: Where is Mary? (W: Mary 在哪兒？)

M: She's at home, I think. We've asked her to go to the cinema, but she won't go with us.

(M: 我想她在家。我們找她去看電影，但是她不跟我們去。)

W: Why not? (W: 為什麼不去？)

M: She says she's seen the film twice. (M: 她說那部電影她看過兩次了。)

W: What's she going to do then? (W: 那麼她要做甚麼？)

M: She is going to stay at home, watching TV. (M: 她要待在家看電視。)

Question: Why doesn't Mary go to the cinema? (問題：為什麼 Mary 不去看電影？)

(A)She doesn't like the film. (她不喜歡那部電影。)

(B)She has seen the film. (她已經看過那部電影。)

(C)She'd like to stay at home. (她想待在家。)

(D)She likes watching TV. (她喜歡看電視。)

答案：(B)

13. W: Excuse me, does this bus go to Shanghai Library?

　　(W: 不好意思，這班公車去上海圖書館嗎？)

　　M: Yes, it does. (W: 是的。)

　　W: Where shall I get off? (W: 我該在哪裡下車？)

　　M: At Huaihai Road. (M: 在 Huaihai 路。)

　　W: Thank you very much. (W: 非常謝謝你。)

　　M: You are welcome. (M: 不客氣。)

　　Question: Where are they talking? (問題：他們在哪裡談話？)

　　(A)In Shanghai Library. (在上海圖書館。)

　　(B)On Huaihai Road. (在 Huaihai 路上。)

　　(C)On the bus. (在公車上。)

　　(D)On the underground. (在地鐵上。)

答案：(C)

14. W: Could you say something about yourself? (W: 你能談談你自己嗎？)

　　M: OK. I left college at the age of 22. Three years later, I was sent to Shanghai.

　　　(M: 好。我二十二歲的時候離開了學校。三年後，我被派到上海。)

　　W: That's in the year of 2002. (W: 那是在 2002 年。)

　　M: No, I came to China in 2001. (M: 不，我 2001 年來中國。)

　　W: So you have been here for a long time. (W: 所以你在這裡已經很長時間了。)

　　M: That's right. (M: 沒錯。)

　　Question: When did the man leave college? (問題：那男人何時離開學校？)

　　(A)In 1998. (1998 年)　　　　　　　　　(B)In 1999. (1999 年)

　　(C)In 2000. (2000 年)　　　　　　　　　(D)In 2001. (2001 年)

答案：(A)

15. M: Would you like to have a cigarette? (M: 你想來根香菸嗎？)

　　W: No, thanks. I've given up smoking. (W: 不，謝謝。我已經戒菸了。)

　　M: It's not easy. I've tried many times, but I failed. How can you make it?

　　　(M: 那不容易。我試了好多次但是都失敗了。你怎麼辦到的？)

　　W: Have you heard an English saying? "Where there is a will, there is a way."

　　　(W: 你聽過一句英文諺語嗎？「Where there is a will, there is a way. (有志者事竟成)」。)

　　M: Oh! You have a strong will. You have set a good example to me.

　　　(M: 喔。你有很強的意志力。你已經為我樹立了一個好榜樣。)

　　Question: Who still smokes? (問題：誰仍然抽菸？)

(A)The man. (那男人。)　　　　　　　　(B)The woman. (那女人。)

(C)Both of them. (兩個人。)　　　　　　(D)Neither of them. (兩個人都不抽。)

答案：(A)

16.　W: What's the matter, Mike? You look upset. (W: Mike 你怎麼了？你看起來很沮喪。)

　　M: I didn't pass the English test. (M: 我沒通過英語測驗。)

　　W: I think you'd better work still harder. (W: 我想你該更努力用功。)

　　M: But I'm not interested in it at all. (M: 但是我一點興趣也沒有。)

　　W: Oh, really? English is an important tool. We must learn it well.

　　　　(W: 喔，真的嗎？英文是非常重要的工具。我們必須把它學好。)

　　Question: Why does Mike look unhappy? (問題：為什麼 Mike 看起來不開心？)

　　(A)Because he worked hard at English. (因為他努力讀英文。)

　　(B)Because he is not interested in English. (因為他對英文沒興趣。)

　　(C)Because he didn't pass the Chinese test. (因為他沒通過中文測驗。)

　　(D)Because he failed in the English test. (因為他英語測驗不及格。)

　　答案：(D)

Ⅲ、Listen to the passage and decide whether the following statements are True (T) or False (F). (判斷下列句子是否符合你所聽到的短文內容，符合的用 T 表示，不符合的用 F 表示。) (7 分)

　　Jean Champollion （1790~1832） was very good at languages. He learnt twelve languages in his life. When he was eighteen, he began teaching history at university. He was younger than many of his students!

　　Jean Champollion （1790~1832）非常擅長語言。他一生中學了十二種語言。在他十八歲的時候，他開始在大學教歷史。他比許多學生還年輕！

　　Jean was very interested in ancient Egypt and in 1821 he began to study the Rosetta Stone. A group of soldiers found this stone at Rosetta when Jean was still a young boy. It was under the sand for hundreds of years before they dug it up. There was a lot of strange writing on the stone. The writing was in three languages. One of the languages was ancient Egyptian. No one could read it at that time. But Jean worked out its secret.

　　Jean 對古埃及非常感興趣，1821 年，他開始研讀「羅賽塔石碑(Rosetta Stone)」。當 Jean 還是個年輕男孩的時候，一群士兵在羅賽塔發現了這塊石碑。在他們把它挖掘出來以前，它已經在沙地底下好幾百年了。石碑上有很多奇怪的文字。這段文字以三種語言寫成。其中一種語言是古埃及文。那時候沒人能讀埃及文。但是 Jean 解出它的秘密。

　　Ancient Egyptian was not a language with letters and words like English. It was full of signs. According to many experts, these signs showed things and ideas. Jean did not completely agree. He thought that some of them showed sounds. He found fifteen signs of this kind in his study of the Rosetta Stone. Today, it is possible to understand ancient Egyptian from 4,000 years ago because of

Jean's discovery.

古埃及文不像英文這種語言有著字母和單字。它充滿了符號。根據許多專家的說法，這些符號表示了事物和想法。Jean 完全不同意。他認為有些符號代表聲音。他在他的「羅賽塔石碑 (Rosetta Stone)」研究中發現了十五種這樣的符號。因為 Jean 的發現，我們現在才可能了解四千年前的古埃及文。

17. Jean Champollion learned about twenty languages in his life.
    (Jean Champolliony 在他的一生中學了約二十種語言。)
    答案：(F 錯)

18. Jean became very interested in ancient Egypt when he was young.
    (Jean 年輕的時候對古埃及非常感興趣。)
    答案：(T 對)

19. Jean started to study the Rosetta Stone in 1921. (Jean 在 1921 年開始研究羅賽塔石碑。)
    答案：(F 錯)

20. Some scientists found the Rosetta Stone under the sand when Jean was a small boy.
    (當 Jean 是個小男孩的時候，一些科學家發現在沙地底下發現羅賽塔石碑。)
    答案：(F 錯)

21. There was a lot of strange writing on the stone. (石碑上有許多奇怪的文字。)
    答案：(T 對)

22. Ancient Egyptian was a language with letters and words like English.
    (古埃及文是一種像英語一樣有字母與單字的語言。)
    答案：(F 錯)

23. Jean thought that some of the signs on the Rosetta Stone told about sounds.
    (Jean 認為羅賽塔石碑上的一些符號表述了聲音。)
    答案：(T 對)

IV、Listen to the dialogue and fill in the blanks.（根據你聽到的對話，完成下列內容，每空格限填一詞。）（7分）

Sun Fei: Hi, Sally. I have some problems with my project on the languages of the world. Will you please help me find some information in your encyclopaedia?

(Sun Fei: 嗨，Sally。我的那份有關世界語言的計畫有些問題。你能在你的百科全書裡幫我找些資料嗎？)

Sally: Sure! What do you want to know?

(Sally: 當然！你想知道甚麼？)

Sun Fei: Well, people around the world speak different languages, right? But how many languages are there?

(Sun Fei: 嗯，全世界的人說著不同的語言，對吧？但是有多少種語言呢？)

Sally: Let me see. Well, there are more than six thousand different languages in the world today.

(Sally: 讓我看看。嗯，現在世界上有超過六千種不同的語言。)

Sun Fei: Which language has the most speakers? Chinese?

(Sun Fei: 哪一種語言最多人說？中文？)

Sally: You are right. There are more than one thousand three hundred million speakers of Chinese. English is the second. There are about three hundred and fifty million speakers of English in the world.

(Sally: 你說對了。有超過十三億人說中文。英文排第二。世界上大約有三億五千萬人說英文。)

Sun Fei: How about the other people?

(Sun Fei: 其他的人呢？)

Sally: Of course, many people speak neither Chinese nor English. Some languages have only a few speakers — about 40 or 50. In some places, only the old people still speak their language. Neither the parents nor the children learn the old language. When grandparents die, the language will die, too.

(Sally: 當然，許多人不說中文也不說英文。有些語言只有少數人說，大約四十或五十人。有些地方，只有老人依舊說他們的語言。父母與孩子都不學那種老的語言。當祖父母過世的時候，那種語言也就死亡了。)

Sun Fei: It is interesting to learn about languages. Thank you for your information, Sally. It is very useful for my project.

(Sun Fei: 認識語言很有趣。謝謝你的資訊。Sally 這對我的計劃非常有用。)

Sally: It is my pleasure!

(Sally: 這是我的榮幸！)

- There are more than __24__ different languages in the world. (世界是有超過___種不同的語言。)
- __25__ is the language with the most speakers（more than __26__ speakers）. (___是最多人說的語言，超過____ 人。)
- __27__ is the second （more than __28__ speakers）. ___ 排第二。(超過___人。)
- Some languages have a few speakers—about 40 or __29__. (一些語言只有少數人說，大約四十或____人。)
- Some languages __30__ when grandparents pass away. (當祖父母輩過世的時候，一些語言也___。)

24. 答案：6,000 (六千)
25. 答案：Chinese (中文)
26. 答案：1,300,000,000 (十三億)
27. 答案：English (英文)
28. 答案：350,000,000 (三億五千萬)
29. 答案：50
30. 答案：die (死亡)

夏朵英文

國中全新英語聽力測驗原文及參考答案

Unit 6

Ⅰ、Listen and choose the right picture.

1. Miss Green has a new car. So she drives to work every day and it saves her a lot of time.
   (格林小姐有一輛新車。所以她每天開車上班而省了很多時間。)
   答案：(F)

2. Mike, look at my new hat. It is a birthday present from my parents.
   (麥克，看看我的新帽子。它是我父母給我的生日禮物。)
   答案：(D)

3. When it snows here in winter, it is really happy to make a snowman.
   (當冬天這裡下雪時，堆雪人真的很快樂。)
   答案：(G)

4. Mary always helps her mother do the housework and now she is doing some washing.
   (瑪莉總是幫助她母親做家事而現在她正在洗東西。)
   答案：(E)

5. Tom and Tim are twins. They are always together after school.
   (湯姆和提姆是雙胞胎。他們放學後總是在一起。)
   答案：(B)

6. I like working with children so I'd like to work as a nurse in a children's hospital.
   (我喜歡和小孩子們一起工作所以我想在兒童醫院當一名護士。)
   答案：(A)

II、Listen to the dialogue and choose the best answer to the question you hear.

7. M: Will you leave at 6.00 or a quarter past six in the morning, Miss Green?
   （男：妳將會在早上六點或六點十五分離開，格林小姐？）
   W: Neither. I'll leave at five to seven. (女：都不是。我將在六點五十五分離開。)
   Q: What time will Miss Green leave? (問題：格林小姐幾點將離開？)
   (A)At 5.45a.m. (上午五點四十五分。)　　　(B)At 6.15a.m. (上午六點十五分。)
   (C)At 6.45a.m. (上午六點四十五分。)　　　(D)At 6.55a.m. (上午六點五十五分。)
   答案：(D)

8. W: Look, Jim. We can park our car here. (女：你看，吉姆。我們可以把我們的車停在這裡。)
   M: Great. Then we don't need to worry about the time to go around.
   　　（男：太好了。那麼我們就不必擔心四處逛逛的時間。
   Q: Which sign are they talking about? (問題：他們正在談論的是什麼標誌？)
   (A)　　　　　　　(B)　　　　　　　(C)　　　　　　　(D)

   答案：(B)

9. M: Alice, why are you at home? Didn't you go for a picnic?
   　　（男：艾莉絲，妳為什麼在家裡？妳沒有去野餐嗎？）
   W: No, it was raining hard and I have to go back home, watching TV.
   　　（女：沒，雨下得很大而我必須回家，看電視。）
   Q: Why does Alice have to stay home? (問題：為什麼艾莉絲必須待在家裡？)
   (A)Because she was late for the bus. (因為她沒趕上巴士。)
   (B)Because the picnic is terrible. (因為野餐很可怕。)
   (C)Because the TV play is interesting. (因為電視節目很有趣。)
   (D)Because it was raining hard. (因為雨下得很大。)
   答案：(D)

10. W: How did your parents like their holiday in Hainan?
    　　（女：你的父母喜歡他們在海南的假期嗎？）
    M: My father thought there were too many people there, but my mother liked it.
    　　（男：我父親認為那邊人太多，但我母親滿喜歡那邊。）
    Q: Did the boy's parents like the holiday? (問題：這位男孩的父母喜歡這個假期嗎？)
    (A)Yes, both of them liked it. (是的，他們都喜歡。)
    (B)No, neither of them liked it. (不，他們都不喜歡。)

(C)His father didn't like it, but his mother did. (他父親不喜歡，但他母親喜歡。)

(D)His mother didn't like it, but his father did. (他母親不喜歡，但他父親喜歡。)

答案：(C)

11. M: What are you going to have for dinner today? (男：妳今天晚餐將要吃什麼？)

W: I have no idea. (女：我毫無頭緒。)

M: Shall we have some fish? (男：那我們要不要吃一些魚？)

W: No. Let's have some meat. (女：不。讓我們吃一些肉吧。)

M: OK. That's a good idea. (男：好。那個好主意。)

Q: What are they going to have for dinner today? (問題：他們今天晚餐將要吃什麼？)

(A)To have some fish. (吃一些魚)　　　　(B)To have some meat. (吃一些肉)

(C)To have some vegetables. (吃一些蔬菜)　(D)To have some chicken. (吃一些雞肉)

答案：(B)

12. W: How about going to the city center? (女：去市政中心怎麼樣？)

M: I'd love to, but I have a lot of things to do. I am too busy these days.

　　(男：我很想去，但我有一堆事情要做。我這幾天太忙了。)

Q: What does the boy mean? (問題：這位男孩的意思是？)

(A)He has been to the city center before. (他以前去過市政中心。)

(B)He is too busy. (他太忙。)

(C)He doesn't like the city center. (他不喜歡市政中心。)

(D)He will not go to the city center. (他不去市政中心。)

答案：(D)

13. M: Did you watch the football match last night, Ann? (男：妳有看昨晚的足球賽嗎，安？)

W: No, I looked after my brother in the hospital. (女：沒有，我在醫院照顧我兄弟。)

Q: Where was Ann last night? (問題：安昨晚在哪裡？)

(A)At home. (在家)　　　　　　(B)In the hospital. (在醫院)

(C)In the library. (在圖書館)　　(D)On the playground. (在遊戲場)

答案：(B)

14. M: What can I do for you? (男：有我可以為您效勞的嗎？)

W: I have a fever and feel terrible. (女：我發燒了覺得很不舒服。)

M: Let me see. Oh, you just have a cold. Take some medicine, and you will be OK soon.

　　(男：讓我看看。噢，妳只是感冒了。服一些藥，妳很快就會好了。)

W: Thank you. (女：謝謝。)

Q: What's the matter with the girl? (問題：這位女孩怎麼了？)

(A)She has a cold. (她感冒了。)　　　(B)She has toothache. (她牙痛。)

(C)She has a cough. (她咳嗽。)　　　(D)She has a stomachache. (她胃痛。)

答案：(A)

15. M: We'll have summer holidays next month. Where are you going?

　　(男：我們下個月要放暑假。妳要去哪裡呢？)

W: I'm going to Chongqing. (女：我要去重慶。)

M: How are you going there? (男：妳要怎麼去那裡？)

W: By plane. (女：搭飛機。)

M: I think it's cheaper to go there by train. (男：我想，搭火車去會比較便宜。)

W: Maybe next time. I've booked the air ticket. (女：或許下次吧。我已經訂了機票。)

Q: How is the girl going to Chongqing? (問題：這位女孩要怎麼去重慶？)

(A)By bus. (搭巴士)　　(B)By train. (搭火車)　　(C)By plane. (搭飛機)　　(D)By ship. (搭船)

答案：(C)

16. W: Dad, I'll be late for school. Could you drive me to school today?

　　(女：爸，我上學要遲到了。你今天可否載我去學校？)

　　M: Sure. But you should get up earlier next time. (男：當然。但是妳下次應該早點起床。)

　　W: Thank you. I will. (女：謝謝。我會的。)

　　Q: What's the relationship between the two speakers? (問題：這兩位對話者的關係是？)

　　(A)Teacher and student. (老師與學生)　　　　　(B)Husband and wife. (丈夫與太太)

　　(C)Father and daughter. (父女)　　　　　　　　(D)Mother and son. (母子)

　　答案：(C)

Ⅲ、Listen to the passage and tell whether the following statements are true or false.

Stephen Hawking was born in Oxford, England on January 8, 1942. He went to school in St Albans. After leaving school, Hawking went first to Oxford University where he studied physics, and then he went on studying in Cambridge University. As he himself says, he didn't work hard. He was a lazy student and did very little work. However, he still got good marks.

史蒂芬霍金 1942 年 1 月 8 日出生於英國牛津。他在聖奧本斯上學。離開學校後，霍金首先去了牛津大學，在那裡學習物理，然後他去劍橋大學繼續就讀。據他自己所說，他沒有用功。他是個懶學生且做很少功課。然而，他仍然拿到好成績。

At the age of 20, he first noticed something was wrong with him. His mother was very worried and took him to see the doctor. He was sent to the hospital for tests. He was ill. The doctor said he would die before he was 23.

在二十歲時，他初次注意到他有什麼不對勁。他的母親很擔憂而帶他去看醫師。他被送去醫院做檢查。他生病了。醫師說他將會在二十三歲前死去。

At first, he became very sad and disappointed. After coming out of the hospital, he suddenly realized that life was beautiful. Later he married, found a job and had three children. He also went on with some of the most important scientific researches.

起初，他變得很悲傷且失望。從醫院出來之後，他忽然領悟到人生是美好的。之後他結婚了，找到工作且生了三個小孩。他也繼續了某些最重要的科學研究。

Today, Hawking still works at Cambridge University as a professor. He strongly believes that his story shows that nobody, however bad his situation is, should lose hope. "Life is not fair," he once said. "You just have to do the best you can in your own situation."

今天，霍金仍然在劍橋大學當教授。他強烈地相信他的故事顯示出無論一個人的境況有多糟，沒有人應該失去希望。「人生不是公平的」他曾說。「你只要在你的狀況下盡力而為。」

17. Stephen Hawking was born in Oxford and once studied in Cambridge University.
   (史蒂芬霍金出生於牛津而且曾在劍橋大學就讀。)
   答案：(T 對)

18. As a university student, Stephen Hawking worked hard and got good marks.
   (身為大學生，史蒂芬霍金很用功且得到好成績。)
   答案：(F 錯)

19. Stephen Hawking first noticed something was wrong with him when he was 23.
   (史蒂芬霍金初次注意到他有什麼不對勁是在他二十三歲時。)
   答案：(F 錯)

20. Stephen Hawking changed his life attitude after he came out of the hospital.
   (史蒂芬霍金在從醫院出來之後改變了他的人生態度。)
   答案：(T 對)

21. Later Stephen Hawking married and there were three people in his family.
   (之後史蒂芬霍金結婚了而他的家裡有三個人。)
   答案：(F 錯)

22. Stephen Hawking did some scientific researches and now works as a professor at Oxford University. (史蒂芬霍金做了某些科學研究而現在在牛津大學當教授。)
   答案：(F 錯)

23. From the passage, we know that we shouldn't lose hope even in a bad situation.
   (透過此短文，我們知道即使在很糟的狀況下，我們也不應該失去希望。)
   答案：(T 對)

IV、Listen to the passage and fill in the blanks.

This message is for Marco Daniel.
這篇留言是給馬可丹尼爾。

My name's David Dolby. I'm sorry I missed your call. I understand that you want some information about the volleyball club. The club meets once a week, on Wednesday evening. Sometimes there are matches on Sunday morning, but those are just for our team players. Our meetings begin at eight, and are about two hours long, so we finish at ten. People like to get home in time for the 10:15 sports program on television. We meet in the Jubilee Hall in Park Lane, behind High Street. The hall doesn't have very good heating, so you'll need to bring a coat to put on afterwards. It's also quite expensive to rent, so our players pay ￡2.75 each week. I hope this answers all your questions and we'll be very pleased to see you at our next meeting!

我的名字是大衛杜比。很抱歉漏接了您的電話。我明白你想要一些關於排球社的資訊。該社團一星期聚會一次，在星期三晚上。有時候星期天早上會有球賽，但是那只是針對我們的球隊選手。我們的聚會八點開始，大約兩小時長，所以我們在十點結束。人們喜歡及時回家收看電視上十點十五分的體育節目。我們在公園路的朱比利堂聚會，在主要大街後面。該堂沒有很好的暖氣，所以您需要帶外套來以便事後穿上。它的租金也頗貴的，所以我們的選手每星期付二點七五英鎊。我希望這回答了您所有的問題，且我們會很高興在我們下一次的聚會見到您！

- Marco Daniel wants some information about the __24__ club.
  馬可丹尼爾想要一些關於排球社的資訊。

- The members in the club meet every __25__ evening.
  該社團的社員每星期三晚上聚會。

- Matches on Sunday morning are just for their __26__ players.
  星期天早上的球賽只是針對他們的球隊選手。

- The meetings begin at __27__, and are about two hours long.
  聚會八點開始，大約兩小時長。

- People like to get home before 10:15 to watch the __28__ program on TV.
  人們喜歡在十點十五分之前回家收看電視上的體育節目。

- They meet in the Jubilee Hall in Park Lane, behind __29__ Street.
  他們在公園路的朱比利堂聚會，在主要大街後面。

- The hall doesn't have very good heating, so Marco Daniel should take a __30__ to put on afterwards.
  該堂沒有很好的暖氣，所以馬可丹尼爾應該帶一件外套來之後穿上。

24. 答案：volleyball (排球)
25. 答案：Wednesday (星期三)
26. 答案：team (球隊)
27. 答案：eight/8 (八)
28. 答案：sports (體育)
29. 答案：High（英國各城市主要大街的普遍名稱）
30. 答案：coat (外套)

夏朵英文

國中全新英語聽力測驗原文及參考答案
Unit 7

Ⅰ、Listen and choose the right picture.（根據你所聽到的內容，選出相應的圖片。）（6分）

A.　　　　　　　　B.　　　　　　　　C.

D.　　　　　E.　　　　　F.　　　　　G.

1.　We are taking a lot of presents with us today because I am hurrying to my grandparents' with my parents. (我們今天帶了好多禮物，因為我趕著跟我爸媽去祖父母家。)
　　答案：(C)

2.　The Lis are having a big dinner together happily.
　　(Lis 全家很開心的在一起吃一頓盛大的晚餐。)
　　答案：(B)

3.　Pigeons on the People's Square are not afraid of people because Shanghainese are always very friendly to them.
　　(人民廣場上的鴿子不怕人，因為上海人對牠們總是很和善。)
　　答案：(G)

4.　Do people still enjoy the beautiful moon on the night of the Mid-autumn Festival nowadays?
　　(現在的人們仍然會在中秋節晚上欣賞漂亮的月亮嗎？)
　　答案：(A)

5.　The students are chatting around the camp-fire at the campsite.
　　(學生們在營地圍著營火聊天。)
　　答案：(E)

6. Would you like to go to the beach with me tomorrow?

(你明天想跟我去海邊嗎？)

答案：(F)

II、**Listen to the dialogue and choose the best answer to the question you hear.**（根據你所聽到的對話和問題，選出最恰當的答案。）（10分）

7. W: Which subject do you prefer, music or sports, Sidney?

    (W: Sidney，你比較喜歡哪一科，音樂還是運動？)

  M: I prefer music to sports. (M:我喜歡音樂多過於運動。)

  Question: Which subject does Sidney like better? (問題：Sidney 比較喜歡哪一科？)

  (A)Maths. (數學。)   (B)Sports. (運動。)

  (C)Music. (音樂。)   (D)Science. (科學。)

  答案：(C)

8. M: The physics problem is very difficult, Mum? (M: 媽，物理問題非常難呢。)

  W: Yes, it may be. Would you like me to help you, David?

     (W: 可能吧。David，你希望我幫你嗎？)

  M: No, thanks, Mum. I'll try to do it myself. (M: 媽，不用了，謝謝。我自己試試看。)

  Question: Why doesn't Tom want his mother to help him?

  (問題：為什麼 Tom 不讓她母親幫他？)

  (A)Tom wants to do it by himself. (Tom 想自己做。)

  (B)Tom doesn't think it's so hard. (Tom 不認為那很困難。)

  (C)Tom is very clever. (Tom 非常聰明。)

  (D)His mother can't work it out. (他母親沒辦法解出來。)

  答案：(A)

9. W: Where have you been? I've looked for you everywhere! (W: 你去哪兒了？我到處找你！)

  M: I was at the school library. I borrowed some books there.

     (M: 我在學校圖書館。我在那兒借了幾本書。)

  W: Are you going to read these books now? (W: 你現在要讀那些書嗎？)

  M: No. I'm going to play basketball with my classmates. (M: 不。我要跟我同學去打籃球。)

  Question: Where was the boy? (問題：那男孩之前在哪裡？)

  (A)At the school. (在學校。)   (B)At the school library. (在學校圖書館。)

  (C)On the playground. (在遊戲場。)   (D)At home. (在家。)

  答案：(B)

10. W: Can I help you? (W: 我能為你服務嗎？)

  M: Yes. I bought this radio two days ago, but it doesn't work. I'd like to change it for another one. (M: 好。我兩天前買了這台收音機，但是它壞了。我想要換另一台。)

  W: Yes. Of course. Have you got your receipt? (W: 當然。你帶了收據嗎？)

M: Yes. Here you are. (M: 帶了。在這兒。)

W: Thank you. Just a moment, please. (W: 謝謝。請稍候。)

Question: What will probably happen finally? (問題：最後可能會發生甚麼事？)

(A)The man got a new receipt. (那男人拿到一張新的收據。)

(B)The man got his radio repaired. (那男人把收音機送修了。)

(C)The man got a new radio. (那男人拿到一台新的收音機。)

(D)The man left there without a radio. (那男人沒帶收音機就離開那兒了。)

答案：(C)

11. W: Is this bike yours, Mike? (W: Mike，這是你的腳踏車嗎？)

M: No, it isn't. (M: 不，它不是。)

W: Whose bike is it, do you know? (W: 你知道這是誰的腳踏車嗎？)

M: Perhaps, it's my sister's. (M: 可能是我姊姊的。)

Question: Who is the owner of the bike? (問題：誰這這輛腳踏車的主人？)

(A)Mike.   (B)Mike's mother. (Mike 的母親。)

(C)Mike's sister. (Mike 的姊姊。)   (D)Mike's father. (Mike 的父親。)

答案：(C)

12. W: What are you doing, George? (W: George 你在做甚麼？)

M: I ... I'm drawing, Miss Li. (M: 李老師，我…我在畫圖。)

W: Oh, yes. What a nice car! But you'd better do it after class.

　　(W: 喔，對。多棒的一輛車。但你最好下課後再畫。)

M: I'm sorry, Miss Li. (M: Li 老師，對不起。)

Question: When does the dialogue happen? (問題：這段對話甚麼時候發生？)

(A)Before class. (上課前。)   (B)During the class. (課堂上。)

(C)After class. (下課後。)   (D)In the classroom. (在教室裡。)

答案：(B)

13. W: Do you often go to school by bus, Peter? (W: Peter，你常搭公車上學嗎？)

M: No, never. I usually go on my bike. But if it rains, my father drives me there.

　　(M: 從來沒有。我通常騎腳踏車。如果下雨的話，我爸爸開車載我去。)

Question: How does Peter go to school on a rainy day? (問題：下雨天 Peter 怎麼去上學？)

(A)By bus. (搭公車。)   (B)By bike. (騎腳踏車。)

(C)By car. (搭車。)   (D)On foot. (走路。)

答案：(C)

14. M: Excuse me, how can I get to the museum? (M: 不好意思，我該怎麼去博物館？)

W: Take a No.71 Bus. It will take you twenty minutes to get there. And the bus stop is five minutes' walk from here. (W: 搭七十一號公車。到那裡要花二十分鐘。這裡到公車站要走五分鐘。)

Question: How long will it take the man to get to the museum?

　　(問題：那男人去博物館要花多久時間？)

(A)Five minutes. (五分鐘。)   (B)Fifteen minutes. (十五分鐘。)

(C)Twenty minutes. (二十分鐘。)   (D)Twenty-five minutes. (二十五分鐘。)

答案：(D)

15. W: Hi, Li Ming, did you take part in the school sports meeting yesterday?

    (W: 嗨，Li Ming，你昨天參加學校運動會了嗎？)

M: Yes, I took part in the 400-metre race. I was third and Wang Pen was second.

    (M: 是的。我參加四百公尺賽跑。我第三名，Wang Pen 第二名。)

Question: Who runs fastest in the race? (問題：誰在比賽中跑得最快？)

(A)We don't know from this passage. (我們無法從這段對話中知道。)

(B)The girl. (那女孩。)

(C)Wang Pen.

(D)Li Ming.

答案：(A)

16. W: Does either of you want a ticket for the science report?

    (W: 你們任何一個想要科學報告的門票嗎？)

M: Why not? Would you like to go? (M: 為什麼不？你想去嗎？)

W: I'd like to, but I've got a lot of things to do for the coming exams.

    (W: 我想，但是我為了下一場考試還有好多事要做。)

Question: Why isn't the woman going to the science report?

(問題：那女人為什麼不去科學報告？)

(A)She's too busy to go.(她太忙以至於不能去)

(B)She's not interested in it. (她沒興趣。)

(C)She hasn't got any tickets. (她沒有票。)

(D)She's ill. (她生病了。)

答案：(A)

Ⅲ、Listen to the passage and decide whether the following statements are True (T) or False (F). (判斷下列句子內容是否符合你所聽到的短文內容，符合的用 T 表示，不符合的用 F 表示。)（7分）

Kelly always wanted to be a scientist. She was interested in maths and physics. She hoped to work in space one day. "I will discover something important in the future," she often told herself.

Kelly 一直想當科學家。她對數學、物理很感興趣。她希望有一天能在太空工作。「未來我將發現重要的事。」她常常告訴自己。

Every evening, Kelly went out with her dog to look at the stars. One night, she saw a strange, coloured light moving across the sky.

Kelly 每天晚上帶她的狗去外面看星星。一天晚上，她看見一道奇特的彩色光芒橫越天空。

"It can't be a star," she thought. "It's too bright. It must be a spaceship! I'm going to see it!" She walked quickly towards the light.

「那不可能是星星。」她想,「那太亮了。那一定是太空船!我要去看它。」她很快地走向那道光。

"The people in the spaceship will want to talk to me. Can they speak our language? Will I be able to understand them? Are they lost?"

「太空船裡的人會想跟我說話。他們會說我們的語言嗎?我會了解他們嗎?他們迷路了嗎?」

The spaceship landed a few metres in front of Kelly and the door slowly opened. Suddenly, Kelly's dog ran towards the spaceship. Kelly cried, "This can't be true!" Two huge dogs stood at the door of the spaceship. The visitors from space were dogs! They said a few words to Kelly's dog. Kelly's dog looked at Kelly and then turned and ran into the spaceship. Then the spaceship was gone.

那艘太空船在 Kelly 前方數公尺降落,門緩慢地打開了。忽然間,Kelly 的狗跑向太空船。Kelly 大叫:「這不可能是真的。」兩隻大狗站在太空船的門口。從太空來的訪客是狗!他們對 Kelly 的狗說了幾句話。Kelly 的狗看看 Kelly,然後轉頭跑進太空船。然後太空船就消失了。

17. Kelly always wanted to be an astronaut to work in space one day.
(Kelly 希望有一天當一名在太空工作的太空人。)
答案:(F 錯)

18. Kelly always thought that she would discover some important things in the future.
(Kelly 總是想著她未來將發現重要的事物。)
答案:(T 對)

19. One night, Kelly saw a strange, coloured light moving across the sky in the park with her dog.
(一天晚上,Kelly 跟她的狗在公園看見一道奇特的彩色光芒橫越天空。)
答案:(T 對)

20. Kelly thought the light was from a spaceship. (Kelly 認為那道光是來自太空船。)
答案:(T 對)

21. The spaceship landed a few metres in front of Kelly. (太空船在 Kelly 前方數公尺處降落。)
答案:(T 對)

22. Kelly was able to understand what the aliens in the spaceship said.
(Kelly 能夠了解太空船上的外星人說什麼。)
答案:(F 錯)

23. Kelly's dog went up to the spaceship and never came back again.
(Kelly 的狗跑上太空船,再也沒回來了。)
答案:(T 對)

Jack: Hello, Mrs. Hu. What's in your hand?

(Jack: 哈囉，Hu 太太。你手裡的是甚麼？)

Mrs. Hu: Oh! Hello, Jack. It's an interesting magazine. It has a report about the future.

(Hu 太太: 喔！哈囉，Jack。這是一本很有趣的雜誌。它有一篇關於未來的報導。)

Jack: Does it say we will live on the moon or things like that?

(Jack: 它是不是說我們將來會住在月球上之類的事情？)

Mrs. Hu: Well, yes. And it also says here people will live in glass houses by the year 2100.

(Hu 太太: 嗯，對。它也說 2100 年我們這裡的人將住在玻璃屋裡。)

Jack: Glass houses? That sounds interesting!

(Jack: 玻璃屋？聽起來好有趣！)

Mrs. Hu: And medicine will cure every illness in the future. People will never get sick.

(Hu 太太: 而且未來的藥物將治癒每一種疾病。人們將不再生病。)

Jack: Then, we'll live longer. What about spaceships? Does it say anything about space?

(Jack: 那麼我們就活得更長了。那麼太空船呢？它提到太空船了嗎？)

Mrs. Hu: Yes, of course! In the future, we'll have holidays in space and live on other planets.

(Hu 太太:當然有！未來，我們將在太空渡假，並且住在其他星球上。)

Jack: It sounds crazy, but fun! I hope it will come true.

(Jack: 這聽起來有點瘋狂，但是太好玩了！我希望那會成真。)

Mrs. Hu: It also says trains are going to be faster. People will travel by train rather than by plane.

(Hu 太太: 他也說火車將會更快。人們將會搭火車而不搭飛機旅行。)

Jack: That's quite strange. We have to travel by plane if we want to go to another country. And planes go much faster than trains!

(Jack: 那太奇怪了。如果我們想去其他國家，我們必須搭飛機旅行。而且飛機比火車快多了！)

Mrs. Hu: Yes, you are right. But planes use too much petrol and the report says we'll run out of it in the future.

(Hu 太太: 對。但是飛機用太多石油，報導說未來我們將用光石油。)

Jack: I see. It's important to protect our environment from now on. Then we'll have a bright future.

(Jack: 我知道了。從現在起保護我們的環境很重要。這樣我們就會有個光明的未來。)

Mrs. Hu: I agree with you.

(Hu 太太: 我同意。)

- People will live on the __24__. They will also live in __25__ houses by the year 2100. (人們將住在____上。他們也將在 2100 年住在____屋裡。)
- __26__ will cure every illness in the future and people will live __27__ than ever. (____將

治癒每一種疾病，人們將活得比以前____。)

● People will have __28__ in space and live on other __29__. (人們將在太空___，並住在其他的___。)

● People will run out of energy sources in the future so people must try to protect the __30__. (未來人們將耗盡能源，所以人們必須試著保護____。)

24. 答案：moon (月球)
25. 答案：glass (玻璃)
26. 答案：Medicine (藥物)
27. 答案：longer (更長/較長的)
28. 答案：holidays (假日)
29. 答案：planets (星球)
30. 答案：environment (環境)

夏朵英文

國中全新英語聽力測驗原文及參考答案

Unit 8

I、Listen and choose the right picture.（根據你所聽到的內容，選出相應的圖片。）（6分）

A.　　　　　　　　B.　　　　　　　　C.

D.　　　　　　E.　　　　　　F.　　　　　　G.

1. Here we are at the Children's Palace. There's a big party today.
   （我們到了幼兒園。今天有一場大型派對。）
   答案：(G)

2. This week Kitty and Helen went to the park for a visit.
   （這個禮拜 Kitty 和 Helen 去公園玩。）
   答案：(C)

3. The boy enjoys surfing on the Internet during the summer holidays.
   （男孩很喜歡在暑假的時候上網瀏覽。）
   答案：(A)

4. I'm going to interview someone who works at the dairy products factory because I want to investigate how milk is made.
   （因為我想調查牛奶是如何製成的，所以我要去訪問一些在奶製品工廠上班的人。）
   答案：(E)

5. I must hurry now. Betty is waiting for me at the entrance to the cinema.
   （我現在得快一點。Betty 在電影院門口等我。）
   答案：(F)

6. Do people in China still play with lanterns on the Lantern Festival?
   (中國人仍然在元宵節玩燈籠嗎？)
   答案：(B)

II、**Listen to the dialogue and choose the best answer to the question you hear.**（根據你所聽到的對話和問題，選出最恰當的答案。）（10 分）

7. M: Were you born in England? (M: 你在英國出生嗎？)
   W: No, I was born in America. (W: 不，我在美國出生。)
   Question: Where was the girl born? (問題：那女孩在哪裡出生。)
   (A)England.(英國。)   (B)China.(中國。)
   (C)America.(美國。)   (D)Russia.(蘇聯。)
   答案：(C)

8. W: How do you go to school every day? (W: 你每天怎麼去上學？)
   M: I go to school by bike. But yesterday I took a taxi to school because it was raining too hard.
      (M: 我騎腳踏車上學。但是昨天的雨下太大了，所以我搭計程車去學校。)
   Question: How does the boy go to school every day? (問題：那男孩每天怎麼上學？)
   (A)By bus. (搭公車。)   (B)By bike. (騎腳踏車。)
   (C)By car. (搭車。)   (D)By taxi. (搭計程車。)
   答案：(B)

9. M: Kally, would you like to have some fish? (M: Kally，你想要來點魚嗎？)
   W: No, thanks. But I'd like to have some spicy sausages, please.
      (W: 不，謝謝。但是請給我一些辣香腸。)
   Question: What does Kally want to have? (問題：Kally 想要吃甚麼？)
   (A)Some rice. (一些飯。)   (B)Some fish. (一些魚。)
   (C)Some meat. (一些肉。)   (D)Some spicy sausages. (一些辣香腸。)
   答案：(D)

10. W: Hi, Jim! What are you doing?(W: 嗨，Jim。你在做甚麼？)
    M: I'm cleaning the floor of my room. (M: 我在清掃我房間的地板。)
    Question: What is Jim doing? (問題：Jim 在做甚麼？)
    (A)Watching TV. (看電視。)   (B)Cleaning the floor. (清掃地板。)
    (C)Reading a book.(讀書。)   (D)Washing the skirt. (洗裙子。)
    答案：(B)

11. W: What did you do last Sunday? (W: 你上星期天做了甚麼？)
    M: I went to see a film. (M: 我去看電影。)
    Question: What did the boy do last Sunday? (那男孩上星期天做了甚麼？)
    (A)He went to the zoo. (他去動物園。)
    (B)He played basketball. (他打籃球。)

(C)He saw a film last Saturday. (他上星期六去看電影。)

(D)He went to the movies. (他去看電影。)

答案：(D)

12. M: How do you go to school every day, Jane, by bike or by bus?

(M: Jane，你每天怎麼去上學？騎腳踏車還是搭公車？)

W: I usually walk to school because my home isn't far away from my school.

(W: 我通常走路去上學，因為我家離學校不遠。)

Question: How does Jane go to school every day? (問題：Jane 每天怎麼去上學？)

(A)By bus. (搭公車。)　　　　　　　　　(B)By underground. (搭地鐵。)

(C)By bike. (騎腳踏車。)　　　　　　　(D)On foot. (走路。)

答案：(D)

13. M: What can I do for you? (M: 我能為你效勞嗎？)

W: I'd like to borrow some story books. (W: 我想要借一些故事書。)

Question: Where does this conversation take place? (問題：這段對話在哪裡發生？)

(A)In the library. (在圖書館。)　　　　(B)At the post office. (在郵局。)

(C)At the supermarket.(在超級市場。)　(D)At the cinema. (在電影院。)

答案：(A)

14. W: I want to buy two cakes and a bottle of milk. How much are they?

(W: 我想買兩個蛋糕和一瓶牛奶。它們多少錢？)

M: A cake costs 2 yuan and a bottle of milk costs 3 yuan. (M: 一個蛋糕兩元，一瓶牛奶三元。)

Question: How much will the woman pay for the food and drinks?

(問題：那女人買食物和飲料要花多少錢？)

(A)5 yuan. (五元。)　(B)6 yuan. (六元。)　(C)7 yuan. (七元。)　(D)8 yuan. (八元。)

答案：(C)

15. M: What day is it today? (M: 今天星期幾？)

W: It's Tuesday. When are we going to visit Shanghai Museum?

(W: 今天星期二。我們甚麼時候要去參觀上海博物館？)

M: Oh, we are going to visit it tomorrow. (M: 喔，我們明天去參觀。)

Question: When are they going to visit Shanghai Museum?

(問題：他們甚麼時候去參觀上海博物館？)

(A)Tuesday. (星期二。)　　　　　　　(B)Wednesday. (星期三。)

(C)Thursday. (星期四。)　　　　　　　(D)Friday. (星期五。)

答案：(B)

16. W: Excuse me, how can I get to the nearest post office?

(W: 不好意思，我該怎麼去最近的郵局？)

17. M: Let me see. Go along this street and turn right into Sun Street. Go on walking and cross the bridge. Then turn left. The post office is just on your right. (M: 讓我想想看。沿著這條街走，然後右轉到 Sun 街。繼續走。過橋後左轉。郵局就在你右邊。)

W: Thank you! (W: 謝謝你！)

M: You are welcome! (M: 不客氣。)

Question: Which one shows the correct route? (問題：哪一張圖是對的路徑圖？)

(A)   (B)   (C)   (D)

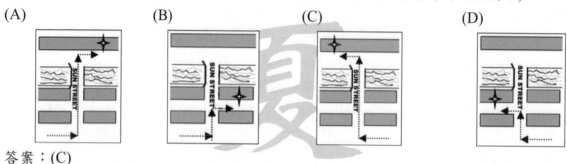

答案：(C)

Ⅲ、Listen to the passage and decide whether the following statements are True (T) or False (F). (判斷下列句子是否符合你所聽到的短文內容，符合的用 T 表示，不符合的用 F 表示。)（7分）

Robot P2 from Honda

Honda's new robot, P2, weights two hundred and thirty kilograms and is two metres tall. It looks like an astronaut. It is the first robot to walk upstairs. It can also push a trolley. Honda made the robot in just 10 months, at a cost of eighteen million seven hundred and fifty thousand yuan.

"People always thought a humanoid robot was impossible," said Professor Sasumi Tachi of Honda. "But P2 shows that it is possible. It can really happen."

P2 cannot think. At least, not for very long. Its batteries run out of power after 15 minutes.

Honda is going to make cars with these robots in the next five years. "The robots will make our cars in dirty and difficult parts of the factory," said Professor Sasumi Tachi. "So our workers will only work in the clean and safe parts of the factory."

When will robots begin to think like humans? Professor Sasumi Tachi thinks it will take millions of years.

來自 Honda 的機器人 P2

Honda 的新機器人 P2，重兩百三十公斤，高兩公尺。它看起來像個太空人。是第一個會上樓的機器人。它也可以推一輛推車。Honda 只花了十個月就完成這個機器人，共花費一千八百七十五萬元。

「人們一直認為人形機器人是不可能的。」Honda 的 Sasumi Taichi 教授說。「但是 P2 告訴大家這是可能的。它真的會發生。」

P2 不能思考。至少，目前是這樣。它的電池在十五分鐘後就耗盡能源。

Honda 將在五年內運用這些機器人來製造汽車。「這些機器人將在工廠裡骯髒又困難的區域製造我們的汽車。」Sasumi Taichi 教授說。「所以我們的工人將只在工廠裡乾淨安全的區域工作。」

機器人甚麼時候能像人類一樣思考呢？Sasumi Taichi 教授認為這將會花上百萬年的時間。

18. P2 is the first robot to walk upstairs. (P2 是第一個會上樓的機器人。)

    答案：(T 對)

19. P2 does not look like an astronaut. (P2 看起來不像太空人。)

    答案：(F 錯)

20. Professor Tachi called P2 "humanoid" because it is like a human. (Tachi 教授把 P2 叫做「人形機器人」，是因為它長得像人類。)

    答案：(T 對)

21. P2 will do some of the work for humans in the next five years. (P2 將在五年內為人類做事。)

    答案：(T 對)

22. P2 can think like a human. (P2 可以像人類一樣思考。)

    答案：(T 對)

23. The robots will work in all parts of the factory. (機器人將在工廠裡的每一個區域工作。)

    答案：(F 錯)

24. It will be a long time before a robot can think like a human according to Professor Tachi. (根據 Tachi 教授的說法，在機器人能像人類一樣思考之前，將是一段很長的時間。)

    答案：(T 對)

IV、Listen to the passage and fill in the blanks. (根據你聽到的短文，完成下列內容，每空格限填一詞。)（7 分）

David Vetter died before he was 13 years old. In his twelve years, he never touched another person!

David Vetter was born with a strange illness. Everything made him sick. Food and water made him sick. The air made him sick. Most things were not clean enough for him. Doctors had to put David in a small plastic bubble and they had to clean everything before he touched it.

When David was small, the bubble was small. There was enough room in it for David and they provided him with many toys. When David grew bigger, his bubble grew bigger, too. There was enough room in it for lots of toys and books. He even had a bicycle. His parents could not touch their son but they could read to him and talk to him through the speaker outside the bubble.

Several scientists studied David's problem, but no one could help him. The plastic bubble made it a safe place for David to live in, since the air inside was cleaner and the water was purer than outside. But it was like a prison. He never got to live a happy life.

David Vetter 在他十三歲之前就死了。他十二歲的時候，他從未碰過任何人。

David Vetter 生來便帶有一種奇怪的疾病。所有東西都會使他生病。食物和飲水使他生病。空氣使他生病。大部分的東西對他來說都不夠乾淨。醫生必須將 David 放在一個小型的塑膠氣泡內，他們要在他接觸之前就要清潔所有的東西。

當 David 還小的時候，氣泡很小。對 David 來說那兒有足夠的空間，他們也給他許多玩具。當 David 長大了，氣泡也跟著變大。裡面就有足夠的空間來擺大量的玩具和書。他甚至有一輛腳踏車。他的父母不能觸碰他們的兒子,但是他們可以從氣泡外的對講機念書給他聽、跟他說話。

雖然有多位科學家研究 David 的問題,但是沒有人能幫助他。那個塑膠氣泡製造了一個讓 David 安全居住的地方,因為內部的空氣比較乾淨,水甚至比外界的還純。但這就像是一個監獄。他從未過著快樂的生活。

● David Vetter was born with a strange __24__.
  (David Vetter 生來就帶有一種奇怪的___。)

● He became __25__ with __26__, water, __27__ and many other things because they were not __28__ enough for him.
  (___、水、___和許多其他的東西都使他___,因為它們對他來說都不夠___。)

● He lived in a __29__ bubble. (他住在一個___氣泡內。)

● He talked to his parents through the speaker __30__ the bubble.
  (他透過氣泡___的對講機跟他父母說話。)

24. 答案:illness (疾病)
25. 答案:sick (生病)
26. 答案:food (食物)
27. 答案:air (空氣)
28. 答案:clean (乾淨的)
29. 答案:plastic (塑膠)
30. 答案:outside (外面的)

夏朵英文
國中全新英語聽力測驗試題
Unit 9

I、Listen and choose the right picture.（根據你所聽到的內容，選出相應的圖片。）（6分）

A.　　　　B.　　　　C.

D.　　　E.　　　F.　　　G.

1. We need to keep calm and quiet when we are reading in the library.
   （我們在圖書館念書的時候要保持安靜。）
   答案：(C)

2. Next program, "Holding our hands together" by the band of five girls called "Beauty" from Class 8E.
   （下一個節目是由 8E 班五個女孩組成的樂團「Beauty」所帶來的：「讓我們一起手牽著手」）
   答案：(A)

3. The two boys are playing computer games excitedly. (那兩個男孩興奮地玩著電腦遊戲。)
   答案：(B)

4. Helen is a good student who likes reading best. (Helen 是一個最喜歡閱讀的好學生。)
   答案：(E)

5. Hey, children. It's midnight. You must stop making noise. Keep quiet, please.
   嘿，孩子們。現在是深夜了。你們不要製造噪音。請保持安靜。
   答案：(D)

6. Children are playing with their crackers and fireworks happily in the yard.
   （孩子們在院子裡快樂地玩著鞭炮與煙火。）
   答案：(F)

7.　M: Where did you go during your holiday? (M: 在假期期間你都做了甚麼？)

　　W: I went to my hometown to see my grandma. (W: 我去家鄉看我奶奶。)

　　M: How old is your grandma? (M: 你奶奶年紀多大了？)

　　W: She's nearly seventy, but she is still very healthy. She loves me dearly.

　　　　(W: 她快七十了，但是她還是非常健康。她非常疼愛我。)

　　M: So you go to see her every year, don't you? (M: 所以你每年都去看她，對嗎？)

　　W: Yes. I always visit her during my summer holiday and winter holiday.

　　　　(W: 對。我都會在暑假和寒假的時候去看她。)

　　Question: How often does the girl go to see her grandma?

　　(問題：那女孩多久去看她奶奶一次？)

　　(A)Once a year. (一年一次。)　　　　(B)Twice a year. (一年兩次。)

　　(C)Three times a year. (一年三次。)　　(D)Four times a year. (一年四次。)

　　答案：(B)

8.　M: It's a fine day today. (M: 今天天氣很好。)

　　W: Yes, a lovely day. Shall we go out for a walk?

　　　　(W: 是阿，多美好的一天。我們去散步好嗎？)

　　M: Why not go skating? It's more exciting. (M: 為什麼不去滑雪？那更刺激。)

　　W: But I'm not good at it. (W: 但是我不擅長。)

　　M: Don't worry. I can teach you and help you. (M: 別擔心。我會教你也會幫你。)

　　Question: In which season are they talking? (D) (問題：他們在談論哪一個季節？)

　　(A)Spring. (春天。)　　(B)Summer. (夏天。)　　(C)Autumn. (秋天。)　　(D)Winter. (冬天。)

　　答案：(D)

9.　M: I'm going to the cinema. There is a new film on today. I hope you can go with me.

　　　　(M: 我要去看電影。今天有一部新電影。我希望你能跟我去。)

　　W: I'd love to, but I'm tired indeed. (W: 我很想，但是我真的很累。)

　　M: You'll have an exam next week, won't you? (M: 你下星期有場考試對吧？)

　　W: Yes. My sister asks me to play tennis with her, but I just want to breathe some fresh air and

　　　　relax myself after a day's hard work. (W: 對。我姊姊要我跟他去打網球，但是我只想在

　　　　一天的辛苦工作候呼吸新鮮空氣和放鬆自己。)

　　M: Then you'd better have a walk in the park. (M: 那麼你最好去公園散步。)

　　W: I think so. (W: 我也這麼想。)

　　Question: Where will the girl probably go? (問題：那女孩大概會去哪裡？)

　　(A)To the cinema. (去電影院。)　　　　(B)To the playground. (去遊樂場。)

　　(C)To the park. (去公園。)　　　　　　(D)To the classroom. (去教室。)

　　答案：(C)

10. M: What's the matter with me? (M: 我怎麼了？)

W: Don't worry. Nothing serious. But I still need to do some tests.
(W: 別擔心。不嚴重。但是我仍要做一些檢驗。)

M: How soon will I be all right? (M: 我多久會好？)

W: In a few days. Here is some medicine. Take a good rest and drink plenty of water.
(W: 幾天之內。這兒有一些藥。好好休息、喝足夠的水。)

M: Can I go to school next week? (M: 我下星期能去學校嗎？)

W: I think so. (W: 我認為可以。)

Question: What is the lady? (問題：那女士是做甚麼的？)

(A)A doctor. (醫生。)　　　　　　　　(B)A teacher. (老師。)

(C)Mum. (媽媽。)　　　　　　　　　(D)Sister. (姊姊)

答案：(A)

11. W: What time will the film begin tonight? (W: 今天晚上電影幾點開始？)

M: It'll begin at six. When shall we start? (M: 六點開始。我們該甚麼時候出發？)

W: After an early supper, at about half past five. Is it OK?
(W: 晚餐後，差不多五點半。好嗎？)

M: I'm afraid the traffic is heavy during the rush hours.
(M: 我擔心在尖峰時間交通會很擁擠。)

W: Then let's set out half an hour earlier. (W: 那麼我們就提早半小時啟程吧。)

M: That's all right. (M: 好。)

Question: What time will they leave for the cinema? (問題：他們幾點離開去電影院？)

(A)At half past four. (四點半。)　　　　(B)At five. (五點。)

(C)At half past five. (五點半。)　　　　(D)At six. (六點。)

答案：(B)

12. M: Have you ever been abroad? (M: 你出過國嗎？)

W: Yes. I have been to America once. I went there in March of 2003.
(W: 是的。我去過一次美國。我 2003 年三月去的。)

M: What did you do during your stay in America? (M: 你在美國的時候做了些甚麼？)

W: I visited a lot of places, such as New York, Washington D.C and so on. (W: 我參觀了好多
地方，像是紐約、華盛頓特區、…等等。)

M: How long did you stay there? (M: 你在那兒待了多久？)

W: About half a year. (W: 差不多半年。)

Question: When did the woman leave America? (問題：那女人甚麼時候離開美國？)

(A)The spring of 2003. (2003 年的春天。)

(B)The summer of 2003. (2003 年的夏天。)

(C)The autumn of 2003. (2003 年的秋天。)

(D)The winter of 2003. (2003 年的冬天。)

答案：(B)

13.　M: I hear that your uncle has been to many countries. Is that true?

　　(M: 我聽說你叔叔去過很多國家。那是真的嗎？)

　W: Yes. He often goes to Japan, America and Europe. He came back from France just last week.

　　(W: 是的。他常去日本、美國和歐洲。他上星期才從法國回來。)

　M: Why does he often go abroad? (M: 他為什麼常常出國？)

　W: Because he is a businessman. He often goes abroad on business.

　　(W: 因為他是一位商人。他常因業務出國。)

　M: Really? He's lucky to make money and go travelling around the world at the same time.

　　(M: 真的？他可以同時賺錢和去世界各處旅行，真幸運。)

　Question: Which foreign country was the girl's uncle in last week?

　(問題：那女孩的叔叔上星期在哪個國家？)

　(A)Japan. (日本。)　　(B)America. (美國。)　(C)Europe. (歐洲。)　　(D)France. (法國。)

　答案：(D)

14.　W: Would you like a cup of tea, Mr. Smith? (W: Smith 先生，你要來杯茶嗎？)

　M: Yes, please. (M: 好，麻煩你。)

　W: With sugar and milk? (W: 要糖和牛奶嗎？)

　M: Oh, no. I'd like Chinese tea with nothing in it, please.

　　(M: 喔不。請給我不加任何東西的中國茶。)

　W: OK. Here you are. (W: 好。給你。)

　M: Thank you very much. (M: 非常謝謝你。)

　Question: Mr. Smith doesn't like Chinese tea, does he?

　(問題：Smith 先生不喜歡中國茶，對嗎？)

　(A)No, he does. (不，他喜歡。)　　　　　(B)Yes, he does. (是的，他喜歡。)

　(C)No, he doesn't. (不，他不喜歡。)　　　(D)Yes, he doesn't. (是的，他不喜歡。)

　答案：(B)

15.　M: Excuse me, but could you tell me the way to Shanghai Zoo?

　　(M: 不好意思，請告訴我該怎麼去上海動物園好嗎？)

　W: Certainly. Go straight and turn left. Shanghai Zoo is in that direction.

　　(W: 當然。直走候左轉。上海動物園在那個方向。)

　M: Should I take a bus? (M: 我可以搭公車嗎？)

　W: Yes. You can take Bus No. 57. It can take you right there.

　　(W: 是的。你可以搭五十七號公車。它會帶你直接到那裡。)

　M: Thank you very much. (M: 非常感謝你。)

　W: You're welcome. (W: 不客氣。)

　Question: How will the man go to Shanghai Zoo? (問題：那男人怎麼去上海動物園？)

　(A)By bus. (搭公車。)　　　　　　　　(B)By taxi. (搭計程車。)

　(C)By underground. (搭地鐵。)　　　　　(D)On foot. (走路。)

　答案：(A)

16. M: Hello! May I speak to Jack? (M: 哈囉！請找 Jack 聽電話。)

W: Sorry, he isn't in at the moment. (W: 抱歉，他現在不在。)

M: This is John speaking. I'm his friend. I have something important to tell him.

(M: 我是 John。我是他的朋友。我有些重要的事要告訴他。)

W: He won't return from school until supper time. May I take a message for him?

(W: 他要到晚餐的時候才會從學校回來。要留言嗎？)

M: Thank you. The film will begin at eight tomorrow. We'll meet at the bus stop.

(M: 謝謝你。明天電影八點開始。我們會在公車站碰面。)

Question: Where is Jack now? (問題：Jack 現在在哪裡？)

(A)In the cinema. (在電影院。)　　　　　　(B)At the bus stop. (在公車站。)

(C)At school. (在學校。)　　　　　　　　(D)At home. (在家。)

答案：(C)

Ⅲ、Listen to the passage and decide whether the following statements are True (T) or False (F). (判斷下列句子是否符合你所聽到的短文內容，符合的用 T 表示，不符合的用 F 表示。)（7 分）

In 1897, H. G. Wells wrote a science fiction book about spaceships coming to Earth. Its name was The War of the Worlds. The book was still very popular in the 1930s. On 30 October, 1938, a man named Orson Welles put out a radio programme from the book. The programme was different from the book in one important way: in the programme the actors talked like reporters and it sounded like a news report to the listeners.

1897 年，H.G. Wells 寫了一本有關太空船來到地球的科幻小說。書名叫做世界大戰。這本書在 1930 年代非常受到歡迎。一九三八年十月三十日，一個叫做 Orson Welles 的人從那本書做出一個廣播節目。這節目和書有一個很大的不同：節目中的演員像記者一樣說話，聽眾聽起來就像是一篇新聞報導。

The actors said, "Space people from the planet Mars are going to attack Earth. Huge things like snakes will come out of spaceships and kill people and people's guns cannot hurt any of them." When people heard this, they were very afraid. Some even left their homes and tried to hide.

那演員說：「從火星來的外星人將要攻擊地球。像蛇一樣的大型怪物將走出太空船殺死人類，而人類的槍完全傷害不了牠們。」當人們聽到了這段節目，他們非常害怕。有些人甚至離家試著躲藏。

Orson Welles waited 40 minutes and later he told the listeners the truth. However, many listeners really believed the news report. They were afraid at first and then they became angry.

Orson Welles 等了四十分鐘，稍後他便告訴聽眾實情。然而許多聽眾仍然相信那則新聞報導。他們起初很害怕，後來卻變得很生氣。

In fact, 30 October is the day before a famous holiday in the USA and some other countries. On this holiday, people play jokes on other people. The holiday is Halloween.

事實上，十月三十日在美國及其他國家剛好是一個著名節日的前一天。人們在那個節日喜歡對人開玩笑。那個節日就是萬聖節。

17. The War of the Worlds was a book about spaceships coming from the Earth.
    (世界大戰是一本關於地球開出的太空船的書。)
    答案：(F 錯)

18. H. G. Wells was the man who put out a radio programme from the book.
    (從那本書做出一個廣播節目的人是 H.G. Wells。)
    答案：(F 錯)

19. In the programme, the actors talked like reporters and the listeners thought it was a real news report. (在節目中，演員向記者一樣說話，聽眾認為那是一則真的新聞報導。)
    答案：(T 對)

20. In the progamme, the actors told the listeners that creatures from other plants would attack the people on Earth. (在節目中，演員告訴聽眾從其他星期來的生物將攻擊地球上的人類。)
    答案：(T 對)

21. No one believed what the actors said on the radio. (沒有人相信廣播上演員所說的話。)
    答案：(F 錯)

22. Orson Welles didn't tell the listeners the truth until 40 minutes later.
    (Orson Welles 直到四十分鐘之後才把實情告訴聽眾。)
    答案：(T 對)

23. It seems that people often play jokes on other people and try to scare them on Halloween.
    (人們似乎常在萬聖節對其他人開玩笑並企圖嚇他們。)
    答案：(T 對)

IV、Listen to the dialogue and fill in the blanks.（根據你聽到的對話，完成下列內容，每空格限填一詞。）（7分）

Liu Mei: Hi, Wang Gang! Do you know this book?
(Liu Mei: 嗨，Wang Gane！你知道這本書嗎？)

Wang Gang: Hello, Liu Mei. Oh, it's The War of the Worlds by H. G. Wells. Yes, I have a copy.
(Wang Gang: 哈囉，Liu Mei。喔，這是 H.G. Wells 寫的世界大戰。是的，我有一本。)

Liu Mei: I think it's a great book.
(Liu Mei: 我覺得是一本很棒的書。)

Wang Gang: I agree! What do you think of his other science fiction books, like The First Man in the Moon?
(Wang Gang: 我同意！你覺得他其他的科幻小說怎麼樣？像是「月球上的第一個人」。)

Liu Mei: I read The Invisible Man when I was a little girl. That's his best book.
(Liu Mei: 我還是小女孩的時候我就讀了「隱形人」。那是他最棒的書。)

Wang Gang: My favourite is The Time Machine.

(Wang Gang: 我最喜歡的是「時光機器」。)

Liu Mei: What's it about?

(Liu Mei: 那是關於甚麼？)

Wang Gang: A scientist builds a time machine and travels to the future. He discovers lots of really interesting things. Hey, maybe you could try to build a time machine!

(Wang Gang: 一位科學家造了一架時光機器去未來旅行。他發現許多有趣的事。嘿，或許你可以試著造一架時光機器！)

Liu Mei: No, I don't think so. I'm more interested in discovering new medicines. They will be more useful.

(Liu Mei: 不，我不這麼認為。我對發現新的藥物比較感興趣。它們更有用。)

Wang Gang: I don't agree. With a time machine, you can travel to the future and just buy new medicines.

(Wang Gang: 我不同意。有了時光機器，你剛好可以去未來旅行買新藥。)

Liu Mei: That's true, but first I need to study for my physics exam.

(Liu Mei: 那是真的，但是首先我要為我的物理考試而讀書。)

Wang Gang: Good luck!

(Wang Gang: 祝好運！)

- Liu Mei and Wang Gang are talking about the following books: The War of the Worlds, The __24__ Men in the __25__, The Invisible Man and The __26__ Machine. (Liu Mei 和 Wang Gang 在討論下面幾本書：世界大戰，___個上___的人、隱形人和___機器。)
- Wang Gang says the book is about a scientist who builds a machine and travels to the __27__. He discovers a lot of __28__ things. (Wang Gang 說那本書是關於一位科學家造了一架機器並且去____ 旅行。他發現許多___的事。)
- Liu Mei is interested in discovering new __29__. She needs to study for the __30__ exam first. (Liu Mei 對發現新___ 很感興趣。首先她需要為___考試而讀書。)

24. 答案：First (首先、第一個)
25. 答案：Moon (月球)
26. 答案：Time (時間)
27. 答案：future (未來)
28. 答案：interesting (有趣的)
29. 答案：medicines (藥物)
30. 答案：physics (物理)

夏朵英文

國中全新英語聽力測驗原文及參考答案

Unit 10

I、Listen and choose the right picture.（根據你所聽到的內容，選出相應的圖片。）（6分）

A.　　　　　B.　　　　　C.

D.　　　　　E.　　　　　F.　　　　　G.

1. Wilson is a hockey player. He has practised playing hockey for about fourteen years.
   (Wilson 是一位曲棍球球員。他練習打曲棍球已經有大約十四年了。)
   答案：(G)

2. It's very difficult to learn windsurfing. But once you try, you'll fall in love with it.
   (學習風帆非常困難。但是一旦你試了，你就會愛上它。)
   答案：(E)

3. Mountain climbing is really a tiring sport. You need to be strong, quite healthy and hardworking.
   (登山是一種非常累人的運動。你需要很強壯、很健康，也要很努力。)
   答案：(D)

4. Wow, boys! Those older students are beating each other on the playground again. Let's go and join them. Take the basketball, Henry. (哇，男孩們！這些高年級學生又在運動場上對抗了。我們去加入他們吧。Henry，帶著籃球。)
   答案：(A)

5. Keep running, Bob and David. You're sure to win. (Bob、David，繼續跑。你們一定會贏的。)
   答案：(C)

6. Although Bob's ankle hurt and he was the last, he still ran to the finishing line with a big smile on his face.

(雖然 Bob 的腳踝受傷了，還是最後一名，但是他臉上仍然帶著大大的笑容跑向終點線。)

答案：(F)

II、Listen to the dialogue and choose the best answer to the question you hear.（根據你所聽到的對話和問題，選出最恰當的答案。）（10 分）

7. W: Look at the snow! (W: 看那片雪！)

M: How beautiful! It snowed heavily last night. (M: 好美！昨晚雪下得很大。)

W: It is thick, isn't it? (W: 雪下的很厚，對吧？)

M: Yes, it is. How about going out and making a snowman? (M: 對。我們來做雪人怎麼樣？)

W: That's great. Let's go. (W: 太棒了。我們走吧。)

Question: What are they going to do? (問題：他們要做甚麼？)

(A)To watch the snow. (看雪。)　　　　　(B)To clean the street. (打掃街道。)

(C)To make a snowman. (做雪人。)　　　　(D)To make a snow ball. (做雪球。)

答案：(C)

8. M: You are not from America, are you? (M: 你不是從美國來的，是嗎？)

W: No, I am from France. (W: 不，我從法國來的。)

M: How long have you learned English? (M: 你學英文學多久了？)

W: For only two years. (W: 只有兩年。)

M: Really? Your English is very good. (M: 真的嗎？你的英文非常好。)

W: Thank you. I'm still trying to improve my English. (W: 謝謝。我還在設法改善我的英文。)

Question: Where does the woman come from? (問題：那女人從哪裡來的？)

(A)America. (美國。) (B)Britain. (英國。)　　　(C)France. (法國。)　　　(D)Britain. (英國。)

答案：(C)

9. W: Hi! I haven't seen you for a long time. Where have you been?

(W: 嗨！我好久沒看到你。你去哪兒了？)

M: I've been to London and stayed there for two years. (M: 我去倫敦待了兩年。)

W: Really? Who did you live with? (W: 真的嗎？你跟誰住？)

M: My brother. (M: 我哥哥。)

Question: What did the man do during the past two years?

(問題：那男人在過去兩年間做了甚麼？)

(A)He went to study in Britain. (他去英國讀書。)

(B)He went to work in Britain. (他去英國工作。)

(C)He went to visit Britain. (他去遊覽英國。)

(D)He went to London and lived with his brother. (他去倫敦跟他哥哥一起住。)

答案：(D)

10. M: Have you ever been to England? (M: 你去過英國嗎？)

W: Yes, I have. I went there in May 2001. (W: 是，我去過。我二零零一年五月去的。)

M: How long did you stay there? (M: 你在那兒待了多久？)

W: Two years. (W: 兩年。)

Question: When did the lady come back? (問題：那小姐何時回來的？)

(A)In 2001. (二零零一年。)   (B)In 2002. (二零零二年。)

(C)In 2003. (二零零三年。)   (D)In 2004. (二零零四年。)

答案：(C)

11. W: Can I help you? (W: 我能為你服務嗎？)

M: Please show me the pink shirt. (M: 請給我看看那件粉紅色的襯衫。)

W: Here you are. That's nice for young girls. (W: 在這裡。這給年輕女孩穿很好看。)

M: Yes, it's pretty. I'll take it. (M: 是的，很漂亮。我買了。)

Question: Where does the dialogue happen? (問題：這段對話在哪裡發生？)

(A)At a shop. (在商店。)   (B)At home. (在家。)

(C)At a library. (在圖書館。)   (D)In a classroom. (在教室。)

答案：(A)

12. M: Hi! Jane. Why are you in such a hurry? (M: 嗨，Jane。你為什麼那麼急？)

W: Hi! Tom. It's ten past two already. I'm going to have an important meeting.
(W: 嗨，Tom。現在已經兩點十分了。我將有個很重要的會議。)

M: When will the meeting begin? (M: 會議幾點開始？)

W: There are only twenty minutes left. (W: 只剩下二十分鐘。)

Question: What time will the meeting begin? (問題：會議幾點開始？)

(A)At ten past two. (兩點十分。)   (B)At two. (兩點。)

(C)At twenty past two. (兩點二十分。)   (D)At half past two. (兩點半。)

答案：(D)

13. W: How much do the fruits cost? (W: 這些水果多少錢？)

M: The oranges, 4 yuan a kilo. The bananas, 6 yuan a kilo.
(M: 柳橙一公斤四元。香蕉一公斤六元。)

W: I'll take two kilos of oranges and one kilo of bananas.
(W: 我要兩公斤柳橙和一公斤香蕉。)

M: The apples are nice and cheap, only 3 yuan a kilo. (M: 蘋果又棒又便宜，一公斤才三元。)

W: OK. I'll take a kilo then. (W: 好。那麼我要一公斤。)

Question: How much will the woman pay for her fruits? (問題：那女人買水果要花多少錢？)

(A)Twenty yuan. (二十元。)   (B)Seventeen yuan. (十七元。)

(C)Eighteen yuan. (十八元。)   (D)Nineteen yuan. (十九元。)

答案：(B)

14. M: What are you going to do after you leave school? (M: 你離開學校後要做甚麼？)

    W: I hope to be a doctor. I'll save people's lives. How about you?

    　(W: 我想當醫生。我要救助人們的生命。你呢？)

    M: I haven't decided yet. Maybe I will be an engineer, like my father.

    　(M: 我還沒決定。我可能會當工程師，像我爸爸一樣。)

    W: My brother is a computer engineer. He likes his work very much.

    　(W: 我哥哥是電腦工程師。他非常喜歡他的工作。)

    M: Really? (M: 真的嗎？)

    Question: What does the boy's father do? (問題：那男孩的父親做甚麼的？)

    (A)A doctor. (醫生。)　　　　　　　　　(B)An engineer. (工程師。)

    (C)A computer engineer. (電腦工程師。)　(D)A teacher. (老師。)

    答案：(B)

15. W: It's two o'clock. The meeting will begin soon. Where is Tom?

    　(W: 現在兩點。會議馬上就開始了。Tom 在那兒？)

    M: He's gone to the library. (M: 他去了圖書館。)

    W: Really? How soon will he come back? (W: 真的？他會多快回來？)

    M: Maybe in half an hour. (M: 大概半小時內。)

    W: Oh, that's too late. We'll begin the meeting without him.

    　(W: 喔，那太慢了。我們不等他就開始會議)

    Question: What time will Tom come back? (問題：Tom 幾點回來？)

    (A)At 2.00.　（兩點。）　　　　　　　(B)At 2.15.　（兩點十五分。）

    (C)At 2.30.　(兩點三十分。)　　　　　(D)At 2.45. (兩點四十五分。)

    答案：(C)

16. M: Where has Mary been for her holiday? (M: Mary 假期去了哪裡？)

    W: She has been to Paris. (W: 她去了巴黎。)

    M: Great! What was the weather like there? (M: 太棒了！那裡的天氣怎麼樣？)

    W: It was sunny. The temperature was 25 degrees. (W: 很晴朗。氣溫二十五度。)

    M: How nice! (M: 真好！)

    Question: How was the weather there? (問題：那兒的天氣怎麼樣？)

    (A)Rainy. (有雨。)　　(B)Cloudy. (陰天。)　(C)Snowy. (下雪。)　　(D)Sunny. (晴朗。)

    答案：(D)

Ⅲ、Listen to the passage and decide whether the following statements are True (T) or False (F). （判斷下列句子是否符合你所聽到的短文內容，符合的用 T 表示，不符合的用 F 表示。）（7分）

David: I'm David. I collect stamps. I have about 1,500 stamps from all over the world. Ben gives me American ones and I get British ones from Sally. Six weeks ago, a boy from Holland gave me some stamps from his country. In my stamp album, I usually put the stamps from each country together. I also collect stamps with sports on them. I put these on a special page. Collecting stamps is fun and interesting.

David:我是 David。我蒐集郵票。我有來自世界各地大約一千五百張郵票。Ben 給我美國的郵票，Sally 給我英國的郵票。六個星期之前，一個從荷蘭來的男孩給我一些來自他的國家的郵票。在我的集郵冊裡，我通常是把來自同一個國家的郵票擺在一起。我也蒐集運動郵票。我放在特殊的頁面。集郵非常好玩也很有趣。

Sally: Hi, I'm Sally. Fishing is fun, too. Fishing takes you to beautiful places. You can catch fish in small rivers, big lakes or the sea. You can go with friends or, if you like, you can go alone. You can make a lot of new friends when you go fishing. You can catch fish with just a net, or with a long piece of string, a hook and some bread. Everybody gets excited when someone catches a big fish. Catching fish is great fun, but eating them is even better!

Sally:我是 Sally。釣魚也很好玩。釣魚會帶你去美麗的地方。你可以在小河、大湖或海裡釣魚。你可以跟朋友一起去，如果你喜歡的話，你也可以自己去。你去釣魚的時候會交到很多新朋友。你可以只靠一個網子捕魚，或者一條長長的線、一個鉤子和一些麵包。當某個人釣到一條魚的時候，大家都好興奮。釣魚太好玩了，但是把魚吃掉更好！

Simon: Hello, everyone. I'm Simon. Making models is my favourite hobby. I have made a few model planes. At the weekend, I fly my planes at a park near my home. If they crash, I have to mend them. I like mending things. It teaches me a lot about real planes. I hope I can work with real planes when I grow up. It is very interesting to make things.

Simon:哈囉。我是 Simon。我最喜歡的興趣是做模型。我已經做了一些模型飛機。周末的時候，我在我家附近的公園放飛我的飛機。如果它們墜毀了，我就要修補。我喜歡修補東西。那讓我對於真的飛機學到許多。我希望我長大的時候，能在跟真的飛機一起工作。製造東西真的非常有趣。

17. David has more than a thousand stamps. (David 有超過一千張的郵票。)

答案：(T 對)

18. David puts his sports stamps with other stamps from the same country. (David 把運動郵票和同一個國家的郵票擺在一起。)

答案：(F 錯)

19. You cannot make new friends when you go fishing, according to Sally. (根據 Sally 的說法，釣魚的時候不能交到新朋友。)

答案：(F 錯)

20. Sally thinks eating fish is better than catching them. (Sally 認為吃魚比釣魚更好。)

答案：(T 對)

21. Simon's model planes sometimes crash. (Simon 的模型飛機偶爾會墜毀。)

答案：(T 對)

22. Simon learns a lot about real planes from mending his model planes.
(Simon 從修補模型飛機中學到很多關於真的飛機。)

答案：(T 對)

23. The three students are talking about their hobbies. (三位學生在談論他們的嗜好。)

答案：(T 對)

IV、Listen to the dialogue and fill in the blanks. (根據你聽到的對話，完成下列內容，每空格限填一詞。)（7分）

David: Did you watch the Manchester United football match on TV last night, Simon?

David: Simon，你昨天晚上看了電視上的曼徹斯特聯盟足球賽嗎？

Simon: Yes, I did. I couldn't believe it. Two goals in the last two minutes!

Simon: 是的，我看了。我不敢相信。最後兩分鐘內進兩球！

David: Nobody could believe it! Five minutes before the end, I said to my dad, "They lost the match!" Then they scored! It was a great match.

David: 沒人相信！結束前五分鐘，我對我爸說：「他們輸了這場球賽。」然而他們卻得分了！這真是一場精采的球賽。

Simon: By the way, David, did I tell you? My dad got two posters of the team for me.

Simon: 另外，David，我跟你說了嗎？我爸給我買了兩張球隊的海報。

David: You're lucky. I don't have any posters of the team.

David: 你真幸運。我一張都沒有。

Simon: Maybe you could have one, if you want.

Simon: 如果你想要的話，你或許可以拿一張。

David: Thanks a lot. I have two good ones of David Beckham. Would you like one of them?

David: 太感謝了。我有兩張 David Beckham 的。你想要一張嗎？

Simon: That would be great. Let's both bring them to school tomorrow.

Simon: 那太棒了。我們明天把它們都帶去學校吧。

Sally: Football! Football! Football! Do you boys think of nothing except watching football and collecting football posters?

Sally: 足球！足球！足球！你們男生除了看足球和蒐集足球海報以外甚麼事都不想嗎？

David: Well, I also have a great new poster of Celine Dion.

David: 嗯，我也有一張 Celine Dion 的大海報。

Sally: Oh! Have you, really? Where did you get it? Can I get one?

Sally: 喔！你真的有嗎？你在哪裡拿到的？我能拿一張嗎？

David: Don't you girls think of anything except singers?

David: 妳們女生除了歌手以外甚麼事都不想嗎？

Some facts about the match by Manchester United (關於曼徹斯特聯盟比賽的一些事)

- __24__ goals took place in the last two minutes. (最後兩分鐘之內射進了___球。)
- First they __25__ and later they __26__. (一開始他們___了，後來他們___了。)

- About posters (關於海報)
- David has got some __27__ posters of David Beckham. (David 有一些 David Beckham __ 的____的海報。)
- Simon has got two posters of Manchester United Football Team from his __28__. (Simon 從他___那兒的得到兩張曼徹斯特聯盟足球隊的海報。)
- Sally wants a poster of Celine Dion and she thinks __29__ only think of __30__. (Sally 想 要一張 Celine Dion 的海報，而且她認為___只想著___。)

24. 答案：Two (二)
25. 答案：lost (輸)
26. 答案：won/scored (贏/得分)
27. 答案：good (好的)
28. 答案：dad/father (爸爸)
29. 答案：boys (男孩們)
30. 答案：football (足球)

夏朵英文

Unit 11

I、Listen and choose the right picture.

A.   B.   C.

D.   E.   F.   G.

1. Do you like playing the violin? (你喜歡拉小提琴嗎？)
   答案：(B)

2. It's very hot today. Tommy has washed his face three times.
   (今天很熱。湯米已經洗了三次臉。)
   答案：(E)

3. Sam, please come to join in our football game. (山姆，請來加入我們的足球賽。)
   答案：(D)

4. Hi, boys. Don't talk when the teacher is giving a lesson.
   (嗨，男生們。不要在老師上課的時候講話。)
   答案：(G)

5. The fisherman can catch many fish on the sea every day.
   (那漁夫每天都可以在海上捕到很多魚。)
   答案：(A)

6. The two girls are dancing happily. (這兩位女孩正快樂地跳著舞。)
   答案：(F)

7.　M: My favourite sport is skating. How about you, Alice?
　　　　（男：我最喜歡的運動是溜冰。那妳呢，艾莉絲？）
　　W: I like swimming best. (女：我最喜歡游泳。)
　　Q: What's the girl's favourite sport? (問題：這位女孩最喜歡的運動是？)
　　(A)Swimming. (游泳)　(B)Running. (跑步)　　(C)Skating. (溜冰)　　　(D)Boating. (划船)
　　答案：(A)

8.　M: Will Betty come to the party, Alice? (男：貝蒂會來參加派對嗎，艾莉絲？)
　　W: Yes, but Sue and Sharon can't. (女：會，但是蘇和雪倫不能來。)
　　Q: Who will come to the party? (問題：誰會來參加派對？)
　　(A)Sue.　　　　　　(B)Betty.　　　　　　(C)Sharon.　　　　　　(D)Alice.
　　答案：(B)

9.　M: Hi, Mary! Is your father a teacher? My father teaches Math at a school.
　　　　（男：嗨，瑪莉！妳父親是老師嗎？我的父親在學校教數學。）
　　W: My father isn't a teacher, but my mother is. She teaches English.
　　　　（女：我父親不是老師，但是我母親是。她教英文。）
　　Q: What subject does Mary's mother teach? (問題：瑪莉的母親教什麼科目？)
　　(A)History. (歷史)　　(B)Math. (數學)　　(C)English. (英文)　　(D)Chinese. (中文)
　　答案：(C)

10.　M: What a sunny day today! Shall we go out for a picnic tomorrow if it is fine?
　　　　（男：今天是多麼晴朗的日子！如果天氣好，明天我們是否該出去野餐？）
　　W: But the weatherman says we'll have rain tomorrow. The weather is so changeable this month.
　　　　（女：但是天氣預報員說明天會下雨。這個月天氣真是多變。）
　　Q: What will the weather be like tomorrow? (問題：明天的天氣會是怎樣的？)
　　(A)Rainy. (雨天。)　　(B)Sunny. (晴天)　　(C)Windy. (颱風)　　(D)Cloudy. (陰天)
　　答案：(A)

11.　M: How many students in your class took part in yesterday's sports meet?
　　　　（男：你們班有多少學生參加了昨天的運動會？）
　　W: Well, there should be 40 students, but in fact only half of them took part.
　　　　（女：嗯，本來應該有四十名學生，但實際上只有此人數的一半參加了。）
　　Q: How many students in the girl's class took part in yesterday's sports meet?
　　　　（問題：這位女孩的班上有多少名學生參加了昨天的運動會？）
　　(A)40.　　　　　　(B)30.　　　　　　(C)20.　　　　　　(D)10.
　　答案：(C)

12.　M: When are we supposed to have the mid-term exam, on Tuesday or Wednesday?
　　　　（男：我們的期中考應該是哪時候，星期二或是星期三？）
　　W: Neither. The headmaster says we'll have the exam on Thursday.

（女：都不是。校長說我們的考試將會在星期四。）

M: That's good. I'll have enough time to prepare for it. (男：那很好。我將有足夠的時間準備。)

Q: When will they have the exam? (問題：他們哪時候考？)

(A)On Monday. (星期一)　　　　　　　(B)On Tuesday. (星期二)

(C)On Wednesday. (星期三)　　　　　(D)On Thursday. (星期四)

答案：(D)

13. W: Hi, Jack! We're supposed to attend a meeting in the city center tomorrow. How shall we go there? (女：嗨，傑克！我們明天應該要在市政中心出席一場會議。我們該怎麼去？)

M: Well, I used to go there by ship, but now I'd rather take a bus. It's more convenient. Besides, it takes less time to go by bus. How about you, Cathy?

（男：喔，我曾經搭船去那裡，但現在我寧願搭巴士。更方便。而且，搭巴士去比較省時間。那妳呢，凱西？）

W: I agree with you. It's both cheaper and more convenient to go by bus.

（女：我同意你的說法。搭巴士去不但比較便宜也比較方便。）

Q: How will they go to the city center tomorrow? (問題：他們明天將怎麼去市中心？)

(A)By ship. (搭船)　　(B)By bus. (搭巴士)　　(C)By bike. (騎單車)　　(D)On foot. (步行)

答案：(B)

14. M: Hi, Carol, I've got two tickets for a football match at the stadium tomorrow evening. Will you go with me? (男：嗨，卡蘿，我有兩張明天晚上在體育館的足球賽的票。妳要跟我去嗎？)

W: Thank you, Paul. But I would rather go to the cinema with my sister. We'll see the American film Avatar. It was a hit in Shanghai last winter. (女：謝謝，保羅。但我寧願和我姊妹去電影院。我們要看美國片阿凡達。它去年冬天在上海大賣座。)

Q: What is Carol going to do tomorrow evening? (問題：卡蘿明天晚上要做什麼？)

(A)Go to the cinema. (去看電影)　　　(B)Go shopping. (去購物)

(C)Go to school. (去上學)　　　　　　(D)Go to the stadium. (去運動場)

答案：(A)

15. M: Jessie, you're a wonderful cook! The fish is really delicious.

（男：潔西，妳是個超強的廚師耶！這魚真的好美味。）

W: I am very glad you like it. Have some more, please.

（女：我很高興你喜歡。請再多吃點。）

M: Thank you. But I am already full. (男：謝謝。但是我已經吃飽了。)

Q: What does the boy mean? (問題：這位男孩的意思是？)

(A)She isn't a good cook. (她不是個好廚師。)

(B)The fish isn't delicious. (魚不好吃。)

(C)He doesn't want to eat more. (他不想再多吃。)

(D)He wants to eat more fish. (他要多吃些魚。)

答案：(C)

16. W: May I help you? (女：我能為您效勞嗎？)

M: Yes, my cousin is graduating from college next week and I'd like to get her a nice gift.

（男：是，我表妹下星期將從大學畢業我想買個好禮物給她。）

W: What price gift are you interested in? We need to know that before we begin looking.

（女：您對什麼價位的禮品有興趣呢？在開始尋找之前我們需要知道這個。）

M: Well, I usually spend about fifty dollars for a gift. Do you have anything nice for that price?

（男：喔，我通常一個禮物花大約五十美金。你有任何好東西在那個價位的嗎？）

Q: Where does this dialogue most probably take place?

（問題：這段對話最可能是在哪裡發生？）

(A)In a library. (在圖書館)　　　　　　(B)In a restaurant. (在餐廳)

(C)In a school. (在學校)　　　　　　(D)In a shop. (在商店)

答案：(D)

Ⅲ、Listen to the passage and tell whether the following statements are true or false.

Hundreds of people have been donating（捐贈） money to a taxi driver, because he found a bag with 32,500 in his taxi and returned it to its owners.

數百名民眾捐了錢給一名計程車司機，因為他在他的計程車上撿到一個裝著三萬兩千五百美元的袋子而將它還給了它的主人。

The donations started after the story was told on the Internet. People were asked to do like the honest driver. So far almost 14,580 has been donated, according to the Internet.

捐贈開始於這個故事在網路上被發布出來之後。人們被要求向誠實的司機看齊。根據網路消息，目前為止已捐出將近一萬四千五百八十美元。

Mr Gray, a taxi driver, found the money after driving an elderly couple. They only went a short distance but they left a bag in the back of his taxi. A few days later he managed to return the bag to its owners. It was an honest story. Everyone was moved. Two young men decided to tell the story on the Internet to thank Mr Gray for his honesty. Now thousands of people have left hundreds of gifts and messages for Mr Gray.

一名計程車司機，葛雷先生，載了一對老夫婦之後發現這些錢。他們只搭了短程但是他們把一個袋子留在他的計程車後座。數天後他設法將它還給了它的主人。這是個誠實的故事。每個人都被感動。兩個年輕人決定在網路上發布這個故事以感謝葛雷先生的誠實。現在數千人留了數百個禮物和留言給葛雷先生。

One visitor gave a snow-boarding lesson to him while another one agreed to give him a second-hand GPS satellite receiver for his taxi. One message said, "I wish more people were like you."

一位訪客送他一堂滑雪板課程而另一位答應給他一個二手的衛星定位接收器讓他裝在計程車上。一則留言寫說，「我希望更多人像你這樣。」

Mr Gray seems a bit confused. He said he only did what had to be done and that he does not quite know what to do with all the things he has been given.

葛雷先生似乎有點困惑了。他說他只是做了應該的事情而不太明白該怎麼處理大家給他的全部東西。

17. Many people are donating（捐贈） money to a taxi driver because of his honesty.
（很多民眾捐錢給一名計程車司機因為他的誠實。）
答案：(T 對)

18. Mr. Gray, the taxi driver, found a bag with 14,580 in the back of his taxi.
（這位計程車司機，葛雷先生，在他的計程車後座撿到一個裝著一萬四千五百八十元的袋子。）
答案：(F 錯)

19. People donated money to Mr. Gray before they learned of the story on the Internet.
（人們在網路上得知這個故事之前就捐錢給葛雷先生。）
答案：(F 錯)

20. The couple forgot to take the bag with them when they got off.
（當那對夫婦下車時忘了把那個袋子帶走。）
答案：(T 對)

21. Mr. Gray found the bag in his taxi and returned it to the couple on the same day.
（葛雷先生在他的計程車上撿到這個袋子且在當天將它還給了那對夫婦。）
答案：(F 錯)

22. People thanked Mr. Gray for his honesty in different ways.
（人們以各種不同的方法感謝葛雷先生的誠實。）
答案：(T 對)

23. This passage is mainly about how to tell a story on the Internet.
（這篇短文主要是關於如何在網路上發布一則故事。）
答案：(F 錯)

Ⅳ、Listen to the passage and fill in the blanks.

Kate Ross is an eighteen-year-old girl in England. Kate left school eight months ago and she will go to university. She loves travelling and decides to visit Asia before she goes to university.

凱特蘿絲是英格蘭的一名十八歲女孩。凱特八個月前離開學校即將要進大學。她喜愛旅行且決定在上大學之前造訪亞洲。

Kate is now living with a family in the capital of Nepal, a small country in Asia. She has learnt a lot about the country since she arrived four months ago. The family has two children but many uncles and cousins live with them in their big house. They have taken Kate to many parties on Friday evenings.

凱特現在和一家人住在一起，在亞洲一個小國尼泊爾的首都。從她四個月前抵達以來她已經對此國家瞭解了很多。這一家人有兩個小孩但是很多叔叔伯伯和堂兄弟姊妹和他們一起住在他們的大房子裡。每個星期五的晚上她們帶凱特去很多派對。

Kate teaches for four hours a day at a small school. All the classes are in English and the students have spoken English since the age of six. The older children speak English very well. Kate has taught writing, grammar and art, all in English. She enjoys art most. And she thinks the children like the lessons best, too.

凱特每天在一所小小的學校任教四小時。所有的課堂都用英文而學生們從六歲起就講英語。較年長的孩子英語講得很好。凱特教作文，文法和美術，都用英文。她最喜歡美術。她認為孩子們也最喜歡這個課程。

Kate has not a lot of time to see Nepal, but soon she will stop teaching and travel around Nepal with a friend. "After that," Kate says, "I will visit more countries in Asia. I'm not sure which ones yet."

凱特沒有很多時間看看尼泊爾，但很快她將要停止教書而和一個朋友一起在尼泊爾四處旅行。「在那之後」，凱特說，「我將造訪亞洲的更多國家。我還不確定哪些。」

- Kate Ross comes from England and she is __24__ years old.
  (凱特蘿絲來自英格蘭，她十八歲。)

- Kate wants to visit Asia before she goes to __25__.
  (凱特想要在上大學之前造訪亞洲。)

- She knows a lot about Nepal and now lives in the __26__ of the country.
  (她對尼泊爾瞭解很多而現在她住在該國的首都。)

- The family has a big house and many __27__ and cousins live with them.
  (這家人有間大房子，很多叔叔伯伯和堂兄弟姊妹們和他們住在一起。)

- Kate has been taken to many parties on __28__ evenings since she arrived.
  (自從她抵達，凱特在每個星期五的晚上被帶去很多派對。)

- Kate teaches writing, grammar and __29__ at a small school.
  (凱特在一所小小的學校教作文，文法和美術。)

- She is not __30__ which countries she will visit.
  (她不確定她將要造訪哪些國家。)

24. 答案：eighteen/18 (十八)
25. 答案：university (大學)
26. 答案：capital (首都)
27. 答案：uncles (叔叔伯伯)
28. 答案：Friday (星期五)
29. 答案：art (美術)
30. 答案：sure (確定)

夏朵英文

國中全新英語聽力測驗原文及參考答案

Unit 12

I、Listen and choose the right picture.

1. Do you still play with lanterns on Lantern Festival in your town?
   (在你的城市你們仍然在元宵節玩燈籠嗎？)
   答案：(F)

2. There are many passengers waiting for the light rail train at the station.
   (有很多旅客在車站等待輕軌列車。)
   答案：(C)

3. How about having a picnic this coming Saturday? (即將來到的這個星期六舉辦個野餐如何？)
   答案：(E)

4. The students are talking about their trip to the Palace Museum happily.
   (學生們正快樂地談論著他們去故宮博物院的旅行。)
   答案：(B)

5. Finally, their little sister burst into laughter after her brother and sister tried for a long time.
   (終於，在哥哥姊姊們試了好久之後他們的小妹笑了出來。)
   答案：(D)

6. Stop making noise, guys! Mr Lin is coming! (停止製造噪音，哥兒們！林先生來了！)
   答案：(G)

7.   W: Hello, Tom. What are you busy doing over there? (女：哈囉，湯姆。你在那邊忙什麼？)

    M: I'm carrying a box to the classroom. (男：我正在把一個盒子搬到教室去。)

    W: What's in the box? (女：那盒子裡有什麼？)

    M: Some books and magazines. (男：一些書和雜誌。)

    W: Do you need some help? (女：你需要幫忙嗎？)

    M: No, thanks. I can manage. (男：不，謝謝。我能搞定。)

    Question: What does Tom mean? (問題：湯姆的意思是什麼？)

    (A)He can carry the box. (他搬得動那盒子。)

    (B)The box is very heavy. (盒子很重。)

    (C)Tom needs some help. (湯姆需要幫忙。)

    (D)He can't carry the box. (他搬不動盒子。)

    答案：(A)

8.   M: What did you do last night? (男：妳昨晚做了什麼？)

    W: I studied English. And I watched TV at the same time.(女：我讀英文。同時我還看了電視。)

    M: How could you do that? (男：妳怎麼做得到？)

    W: It was very easy. The film on TV was in English.

       (女：很簡單。電視所播出的電影是英文的。)

    M: Well done. I'll try next time, too. (男：做得好。下次我也來試試。)

    Question: What did the girl do last night? (問題：這位女生昨晚做了什麼？)

    (A)She studied English and then watched TV. (她先讀英文再看電視。)

    (B)She studied English instead of watching TV. (她讀英文沒有看電視。)

    (C)She watched TV after she studied English. (她看完電視後讀英文。)

    (D)She studied English by watching TV. (她看電視學英文。)

    答案：(D)

9.   W: Hi, Tom. Where are you going? (女：嗨，湯姆。你要去哪裡？)

    M: I'm going to the cinema. What time is it by your watch?

       (男：我正要去電影院。妳的手錶幾點？)

    W: It's half past two. (女：兩點半。)

    M: Oh! There are only fifteen minutes left. My watch is ten minutes slow. I must hurry. See you

       later. (男：噢！只剩下十五分鐘了。我的手錶慢了十分鐘。我得趕快。回頭見。)

    Question: What time will the film begin? (問題：電影幾時將開演？)

    (A)2.30.   (B)2.40.   (C)2.45.   (D)3.00.

    答案：(C)

10. M: Where had you lived before you moved to Shanghai? (男：妳搬到上海之前住在哪裡？)

    W: In Nanjing. (女：在南京。)

    M: I went to Nanjing last summer. I don't like it. It's too hot in summer.

（男：去年夏天我去了南京。我不喜歡。那邊夏天太熱了。）

W: Oh, I do. There are more trees there than here.

（女：喔，我挺喜歡的。那邊比這邊有更多樹木。）

M: But why have you moved here? (男：但是妳為什麼搬過來這邊？)

W: I have got a better job in Shanghai. (女：我在上海得到一個較好的工作。)

Question: Who likes Nanjing? (問題：誰喜歡南京？)

(A)The man. (男士)　　　　　　　　(B)The woman. (女士)

(C)Both of them. (都喜歡)　　　　(D)Neither of them. (都不喜歡)

答案：(B)

11. W: It's a pity! The film was just over. Tom, where have you been?

（女：好可惜！電影剛結束。湯姆，你去了哪裡啊？）

M: I've been to school. Professor Yang made a speech this morning.

（男：我去了學校。楊教授今天早上發表了一場演講。）

W: Really? What was it about? (女：真的？是講什麼的？)

M: It was about space science. It's very interesting. (男：是講太空科學的。很有意思。)

W: I'm interested in space science, too. (女：我也對太空科學有興趣。)

Question: Why did the boy go to school? (問題：這位男生為什麼去學校？)

(A)To have a talk. (去談話。)　　　　(B)To have an English lesson. (上英文課。)

(C)To attend a lecture. (去聽演講。)　　(D)To play football. (去踢足球。)

答案：(C)

12. M: Hi! Jane. What are you doing now? (男：嗨！珍。妳現在正在做什麼？)

W: I'm reading a book. Could you tell me what this word means?

（女：我正在讀一本書。你可以告訴我這個字的意義嗎？）

M: Sorry, I don't know its meaning. (男：抱歉，我不知道它的意義。)

W: What can I do? (女：我能怎麼辦？)

M: Why not look it up in the dictionary? I have got a good dictionary.

（男：何不在字典裡查一查？我有一本好字典。）

W: Good idea. (女：好主意。)

Question: What are they going to do soon? (問題：他們即將做什麼？)

(A)To buy a dictionary. (買字典)

(B)To look up the word in the dictionary. (在字典裡查那個單字)

(C)To borrow a dictionary. (借字典)

(D)To ask the teacher for help. (請老師幫忙)

答案：(B)

13. W: What time is it now? (女：現在幾點？)

M: About half past four. It's still early. (男：大約四點半。還早。)

W: I'm afraid I must go now. (女：我恐怕必須現在離開。)

M: Why are you in such a hurry? Can't you stay for supper?

(男：妳為何如此匆忙？妳不能留下來用晚餐嗎？)

W: Thank you for your kindness, but I must buy some vegetables for supper before my son comes home from school.

（女：謝謝你的好意，但我必須在我兒子從學校回家之前買些晚餐要吃的蔬菜。）

Question: Where is the woman going now? (問題：這位女士現在要去哪裡？)

(A)To her office. (去辦公室)

(B)To school. (去學校)

(C)To the market. (去市場)

(D)To stay for supper. (在家做晚餐)

答案：(C)

14. M: Hi, Mary. I hear your school library is very large. Can you tell me something about it?

（男：嗨，瑪莉。我聽說妳學校的圖書館很大。妳可以告訴我一些關於它的事嗎？）

W: Certainly. What would you like to know? (女：當然。你想知道些什麼？)

M: How many books have you got? (男：你們有多少本書？)

W: About 40,000 altogether. Some are Chinese, and others are English.

（女：總共大約四萬本。有些是中文的，而其它是英文的。）

M: How many English books? (男：有多少英文書？)

W: About a quarter of the total. (女：大約總數的四分之一。)

Question: How many English books are there in the school's library?

（問題：在此校的圖書館裡有多少本英文書？）

(A)40,000.　　　　(B)30,000.　　　　(C)20,000.　　　　(D)10,000.

答案：(D)

15. M: I'd like to eat some chocolate, Mum. (男：我想要吃些巧克力，媽媽。)

W: I'm afraid you can't. You always have too much of it. It's bad for your teeth.

（女：我恐怕你不行喔。你總是吃太多。它對你的牙齒不好。）

M: But I will brush my teeth before going to bed. (男：但是我在睡前會刷牙啊。)

W: You'll become fatter and fatter. (女：你將會變得愈來愈胖。)

M: What else can I eat then? (男：那麼還有什麼其它我可以吃的？)

W: You'd better eat more fruit and vegetables. They are good for your health.

（女：你最好多吃些水果和蔬菜。它們對你的健康有益。）

Question: What does the boy usually like to eat? (問題：這個男孩通常喜歡吃什麼？)

(A)Some chicken. (雞肉)　　　　　　　　(B)Some chocolate. (巧克力)

(C)Some fruit. (水果)　　　　　　　　　(D)Some vegetables. (蔬菜)

答案：(B)

16. W: Mike, you didn't come to school yesterday. Was there anything wrong?

（女：麥克，你昨天沒來學校。有什麼狀況嗎？）

M: Yes, I had a bad cold. The doctor told me to stay in bed for at least one day.

（男：有，我重感冒。醫師要我至少在床上待一天。）

W: I'm sorry to hear that. How are you today? (女：我很遺憾聽到這消息。你今天如何？)

M: Much better, thank you. The headmaster told me you gave the lessons to my students yesterday. It's very kind of you.

（男：好多了，謝謝。校長告訴我妳昨天幫我的學生上了課。妳真好心。）

W: It's my pleasure. (女：我很樂意的。)

Question: What is Mike? (問題：麥克的職業是？)

(A)The doctor. (醫生)　　　　　　　　　(B)The headmaster. (主任)

(C)The teacher. (老師)　　　　　　　　　(D)The student. (學生)

答案：(C)

Ⅲ、Listen to the passage and decide whether the following statements are True (T) or False (F).

You will love beautiful San Francisco!

你會愛上美麗的舊金山！

San Francisco Bay is a harbour of bright blue water. To look down on the bay, travel up the highest hill by cable car. Of course, you can also walk, but you will need strong legs! It is never too hot and never too cold here. Sports-lovers can come and watch American football or baseball games. Food-lovers will find delicious fish and other seafood at our great restaurants.

舊金山灣是個有湛藍海水的港口。要俯瞰海灣，就搭纜車上最高的山丘。當然，你也可以徒步，但你會需要強壯的雙腿！這裡的天氣從不會太熱也從不會太冷。運動愛好者可以來觀賞美式足球或棒球賽。美食愛好者可以在我們絕讚的餐廳裡找到美味的魚和其他海鮮。

Enjoy the California sunshine!

享受加州的陽光！

See the famous Golden Gate Bridge. Cross the bridge to Golden Gate Park, with its beautiful lakes, trees and gardens. In the park you can fish, walk or play tennis. When you need a rest, come and have something to eat and drink in our Japanese Tea Garden. Nothing could be nicer!

看看著名的金門大橋。過橋到金門公園，它有著美麗的湖泊、樹和花園。在公園裡你可以釣魚、散步或打網球。當你需要休息，來我們的日本茶花園吃喝點東西吧。沒有更棒的事了！

Spend Chinese New Year's Day

歡度中國新年

Here! For a Chinese New Year's Day with a difference, come to San Francisco and take part in our wonderful festival. San Francisco's Chinatown is the largest outside Asia. Behind its big green gate, you will find all kinds of food from China, and many warm welcomes.

來！想度過一個與眾不同的中國新年，來舊金山參加我們精彩的慶典。舊金山的中國城是在亞洲以外最大規模的。在它巨大的綠色大門後，你將找到各種來自中國的食物和許多熱烈的歡迎。

17. San Francisco is a cold, dark place.(舊金山是個寒冷、陰暗的地方。)

答案：(F 錯)

18. According to the passage, it is a long way to walk to the top of the hill if you want to look down on San Francisco Bay.(根據此文，如果你想俯瞰舊金山灣的話徒步上山丘頂的路很長。)

答案：(T 對)

19. Only sports-lovers or food-lovers should visit San Francisco.(只有運動愛好者或美食愛好者該造訪舊金山。)

答案：(T 對)

20. Golden Gate Park is near Golden Gate Bridge.(金門公園靠近金門大橋。)

答案：(T 對)

21. You can find a Japanese Tea Garden in the Golden Gate Park.

(你可以在金門公園內找到日本茶花園。)

答案：(T 對)

22. In Chinatown you can only get hot Sichuan food. (在中國城你只能買到辣的四川料理。)

答案：(F 錯)

23. San Francisco's Chinatown is bigger than London's. (舊金山的中國城比倫敦的更大。)

答案：(T 對)

Ⅳ、Listen to the passage and fill in the blanks.

Today, I am going to talk about Bangkok, my hometown and the capital of my country, Thailand. There are many interesting places to visit in Bangkok, but first I want to tell you about our traffic problem.

今天，我將和大家談談曼谷，我的家鄉並且是我國泰國的首都。曼谷有很多可參觀的有趣所在，但首先我想告訴各位關於我們的交通問題。

The streets are very crowded in Bangkok, so it can take a long time to get from place to place. It used to take me more than two hours to get to school by bus! I often slept on my way there!

在曼谷的街道非常擁擠，所以從一處到另一處可能要很長時間。我曾經需要花超過兩小時搭公車上學！在那邊我經常在路途中睡覺！

If you want to get somewhere on time in Bangkok, you must leave early. Lots of people take tuk-tuks to get through the traffic quickly. Tuk-tuks are like little cars with three wheels.

如果你想在曼谷準時到達某處，你必須提早出發。很多人搭嘟嘟車快速通過塞車。嘟嘟車像有三個輪子的小汽車。

Bangkok is next to a big river. It is interesting to visit the Floating Market on the river. At the market, people sell lots of fresh fruit and vegetables from their boats.

曼谷緊鄰一條大河。參觀河上的水上市場很有趣。在市場裡，人們從他們的船上販賣大量的新鮮水果和蔬菜。

In November, we have the Festival of Lights. Everyone makes lights during the festival. Then, after dark, we put them carefully into the river and watch them sail away. It is beautiful to see the river with millions of little lights on it.

十一月時，我們有點燈節。在此節日每個人都製作燈飾。接著，天黑後，我們小心地把它們放到河裡看著它們漂走。看著河上百萬盞小燈光很美。

Thailand is also famous for its food. Thai food is very hot like some Chinese food. So if you like Sichuan food, you'll love Thai food!

泰國也以它的美食著名。泰式料理像一些中國料理一樣很辣。所以如果你喜歡四川菜，你也會愛上泰國菜！

Many thanks, everyone, for listening to me.

多謝各位聽我講述。

- Streets in Bangkok are __24__
  (曼谷的街道擁擠。)
- People must leave __25__ if they go to work in the morning.
  (如果他們早上去上班，人們必須提早出發。)
- Tuk-tuks are like little __26__ with __27__ wheels
  (嘟嘟車像有三個輪子的小汽車。)
- Bangkok is famous for its Floating __28__
  (曼谷以它的水上市場而著名。)
- People sell fruit and vegetables from their __29__
  (人們從他們的船上販賣水果和蔬菜。)
- Thai food are usually very __30__
  (泰國料理通常很辣。)

24. 答案：crowded (擁擠)
25. 答案：early (早)
26. 答案：cars (汽車)
27. 答案：three/3 (三)
28. 答案：Market (市場)
29. 答案：boats (船)
30. 答案：hot (辣)

夏朵英文
國中全新英語聽力測驗原文及參考答案
Unit 13

I、Listen and choose the right picture.

A.　　　　　　　　B.　　　　　　　　C.

D.　　　　　E.　　　　　F.　　　　　G.

1.　Hey, Jack. Bring my trousers to me! (嘿，傑克。把我的長褲拿給我。)
　　答案：(G)

2.　The British often have some tea and snacks at teatime in the afternoon.
　　(英國人經常在下午的午茶時間用些茶和點心。)
　　答案：(B)

3.　It is common to see people playing golf in big cities in China these days.
　　(現在在中國的大都市看到人們打高爾夫球是很普遍的。)
　　答案：(D)

4.　Sir, are there any tickets for the movie Red Cliff left? I want two.
　　(先生，電影紅色懸崖的票還有任何剩下的嗎？我想要兩張。)
　　答案：(E)

5.　Look at the happy couple. They got married in the church just now.
　　(看那對快樂的夫婦。他們剛剛才在教堂結了婚。)
　　答案：(A)

6.　Dear, our Christmas turkey is OK. Have a try, please!
　　(親愛的，我們的聖誕火雞還不錯。請嚐嚐看！)
　　答案：(F)

7.　M: What do you need for your birthday, a dictionary or a camera?

　　（男：妳生日禮物需要什麼，一本字典或一台相機。）

　　W: Neither. I need a walkman to listen to English. (女：都不是。我需要一台隨身聽來聽英語。)

　　M: What else do you want? (男：妳還想要什麼其他的？)

　　W: Some English tapes. (女：一些英語錄音帶。)

　　Question: What does the girl want for her birthday? (問題：這個女孩想要什麼生日禮物？)

　　(A)A walkman and some English tapes.　　　(B)A dictionary.

　　(C)Some music tapes.　　　(D)A camera and a dictionary.

　　答案：(A)

8.　M: Jane, are you taller than Mike? (男：珍，妳比麥克高嗎？)

　　W: Yes, I'm 10 centimetres taller than he. (女：是的，我比他高十公分。)

　　M: Then you must be the tallest in your class. (男：那麼妳一定是妳的班上最高的囉。)

　　W: No, Tom and David are much taller than I. Tom is 1.75 metres and David is 1.80 metres.

　　　（女：不是，湯姆和大衛比我高得多。湯姆有一點七五公尺而大衛有一點八公尺。）

　　Question: Who is the tallest in his class? (問題：在他的班上誰最高？)

　　(A)Mike.　　　(B)Tom.　　　(C)David.　　　(D)Jane.

　　答案：(C)

9.　W: Let me introduce my class to you. What do you want to know about?

　　　（女：讓我來向你介紹我的班級。你想知道些什麼？）

　　M: How many students are there in your class? (男：妳的班上有幾名學生？)

　　W: There are fifty. Two-fifths of the students are boys.

　　　（女：有五十名。學生中的五分之二是男生。）

　　Question: How many girls are there in the class? (問題：這班上有多少名女生？)

　　(A)Fifty-two. (52)　　(B)Twenty. (20)　　(C)Fifty. (50)　　(D)Thirty. (30)

　　答案：(D)

10.　M: I remember seeing you somewhere. Perhaps at the airport or at the railway station.

　　　（男：我記得在某處見過妳。或許是在機場或在火車站。）

　　W: You helped me with my bags in the underground and then you took me to the bus stop.

　　　（女：你在地鐵幫我提袋子然後你帶我去公車站。）

　　Question: Where did they first meet? (問題：他們第一次見面是在哪裡？)

　　(A)At a bus stop. (公車站)　　　(B)In the underground. (地鐵)

　　(C)At the railway station. (火車站)　　　(D)At the airport. (機場)

　　答案：(B)

11.　M: You've got your telephone now, haven't you? (男：妳現在有自己的電話了，對吧？)

　　W: Yes, I have. (女：對，我有。)

　　M: What's your telephone number? (男：妳的電話號碼幾號？)

W: It's 65750853. What's yours? (女：65750853。 你的呢？)

M: Mine is 65758053. (男：我的是 65758053。)

Question: What is the man's telephone number? (問題：這位男士的電話號碼幾號？)

(A)65758053.　　　　(B)65750853.　　　　(C)65758035.　　　　(D)65750835.

答案：(A)

12. M: Look! How beautiful the white world is! (男：看啊！白色世界是多麼地美麗！)

W: It snowed heavily last night. It's hard to go to work by bike. You'd better take a bus today.

　　(女：昨晚下了很大的雪。騎腳踏車上班很困難。你今天最好搭公車。)

Question: How does the man usually go to work? (問題：這位男士通常如何去上班？)

(A)By taxi. (坐計程車)　　　　　　　　(B)By bike. (騎單車)

(C)By bus. (搭公車)　　　　　　　　　(D)On foot. (步行)

答案：(B)

13. M: What do you usually do when you are free? (男：當妳空閒的時候通常做什麼？)

W: I usually sing songs and play the piano. I go to the beach very often.

　　(女：我通常唱歌和彈鋼琴。我很常去海灘。)

M: I like playing the piano. But I spend more time watching football match.

　　(男：我喜歡彈鋼琴。但是我花更多時間看足球賽。)

Question: Does the girl like watching TV or singing songs?

　　(問題：這位女孩喜歡看電視還是唱歌？)

(A)Yes, she does. (是的，她喜歡。)

(B)No, she doesn't. (不，她不喜歡。)

(C)She likes singing songs. (她喜歡唱歌。)

(D)She likes watching TV. (她喜歡看電視。)

答案：(C)

14. W: John, I have to leave now. (女：約翰，我現在必須離開。)

M: Why? It's still early. (男：為什麼？還早啊。)

W: I'm sorry. I must catch the 10.55 bus. (女：我很抱歉。我必須趕上十點五十五分的公車。)

M: But it is only a quarter to ten. Please stay a little longer.

　　(男：但現在才九點四十五分。請多待一會兒。)

Question: What time is it now? (問題：現在幾點？)

(A)9.45.　　　　(B)11.05.　　　　(C)10.15.　　　　(D)10.55.

答案：(A)

15. M: Where did you go, Alice? (男：妳去了哪裡，艾莉絲？)

W: I went to the countryside. (女：我去了鄉下。)

M: Who did you go to visit? (男：妳是去看誰？)

W: I went to visit my grandmother. I go to visit her once three months.

　　(女：我去看我祖母。我每三個月會去看她一次。)

Question: How often does she go to visit her grandmother? (問題：她有多常去拜訪她祖母？)

(A)Four times a year. (一年四次)　　　(B)Four times a month. (一個月四次)

(C)Three times a month. (一個月三次)　　(D)Once every six months. (六個月一次)

答案：(A)

16. W: Would you like a cup of coffee, Simon? (女：你想要來一杯咖啡嗎，賽門？)

M: Yes, please. (男：好，麻煩妳。)

W: With milk or sugar? (女：加奶或糖？)

M: No, thanks. (男：不用，謝謝。)

Question: What kind of coffee does Simon want? (問題：賽門想要哪一種咖啡？)

(A)Black coffee. (黑咖啡)

(B)Coffee with sugar and milk. (加糖和牛奶的咖啡)

(C)Coffee with sugar. (咖啡加糖)

(D)Coffee with milk. (咖啡加牛奶)

答案：(A)

Ⅲ、Listen to the passage and decide whether the following statements are True (T) or False (F).

Dear friends,

親愛的朋友們，

Trees are our friends. They work hard for us. They cool our cities and clean the air. They also give out oxygen for us to breathe. Trees reduce sound pollution in cities and make cities more beautiful.

樹木是我們的朋友。它們為我們努力工作。它們為我們的都市降溫並清淨空氣。它們也給我們氧氣讓我們呼吸。樹木降低都市中的噪音污染使都市更美麗。

Trees provide a lot of things for people. They provide food. They also supply material for houses, furniture and paper products. Some trees even provide important ingredients for medicine. Without trees, the soil would be washed away and there would be no food for us to eat. Without trees, it would get too hot for us to live on Earth. Without trees, we would die.

樹木為人們提供很多東西。它們提供食物。它們也供應房屋的建材、傢俱和紙類產品。有些樹甚至提供藥品中的重要成分。沒有了樹木，土壤會被沖刷走且我們也會沒有食物可吃。沒有了樹木，地球會熱得讓我們無法居住。沒有了樹木，我們會死。

In the last 200 years, more than half of all the trees on Earth have been destroyed. We need more trees!

在過去的兩百年中，地球上超過一半的樹木被毀滅。我們需要更多樹木！

Trees for Earth is making a difference. To help protect our environment, we plant trees and take care of them. We need more people to join us in this project.

「給地球種樹」正在改變這局面。為了幫助保護我們的環境，我們栽種樹木並且照顧它們。我們需要更多人加入我們這個行動。

We want to plant 100 million trees in the next 10 years. If you want to find out more about us, please send us an e-mail at info@treesforearth.org.

我們想要在未來的十年之中栽種一億棵樹。如果妳想要知道更多關於我們的事，請寄電郵到 info@treesforearth.org 給我們。

From
來自
Trees for Earth
給地球種樹

17. Trees cool the cities as well as clean the air. (樹木為我們的都市降溫並清淨空氣。)
    答案：(T)

18. Trees can reduce sound pollution and make cities beautiful.
    (樹木可以降低都市中的噪音污染使都市更美麗。)
    答案：(T)

19. We sometimes can use certain kinds of trees to make medicine.
    (我們有時候可以用某些特定種類的樹來製作藥品。)
    答案：(T)

20. When we grow trees, soil in the ground will be washed away.
    (當我們種樹，地上的土壤將被沖刷走。)
    答案：(F)

21. In the last 200 years, about 3/4 of the trees on Earth were destroyed.
    (在過去的兩百年中，地球上大約四分之三的樹木被摧毀。)
    答案：(F)

22. Trees for Earth is an organization for protecting trees all over the world.
    (給地球種樹是一個保護全世界樹木的組織。)
    答案：(T)

23. The e-mail address of Trees for Earth is info@treesforearth.com.
    (給地球的樹的電郵信箱是info@treesforearth.com。)
    答案：(F)

Ⅳ、Listen to the dialogue and fill in the blanks.

Ben: How did you and your friends travel around China? By bike?
     (班：妳和妳朋友如何在中國旅行的？騎腳踏車？)

Emma: Oh, no! We rode around the countryside on buses and took trains at several places along the way.
      (艾瑪：喔，不！我們搭巴士在鄉間四處遊覽且沿途在數個地方搭火車。)

Ben: Which place did you go to first? (班：妳們最先去了哪個地方？)

Emma: We went to Beijing first. It's the capital of China. We visited many interesting places there. (艾瑪：我們最先去了北京。它是中國的首都。在那邊我們拜訪了很多有趣的地方。)

Ben: It sounds great. Five years ago, I went to Beijing with my parents. We were caught in a sandstorm. It was difficult to breathe and the sand even hurt us. Were you caught in a sandstorm in Beijing?

(班：聽起來很棒。五年前，我和我父母去了北京。我們遇到一場沙塵暴。呼吸困難而且沙子甚至傷害到我們。妳在北京有遇到沙塵暴嗎？)

Emma: No, we weren't. There are fewer sandstorms than before. Now people are trying to stop the sandstorms by planting more trees. Trees help hold the sand and soil together and stop them from being blown away.

(艾瑪：沒，我們沒有。沙塵暴沒有之前那樣多了。現在人們試著種植更多樹來阻止沙塵暴。樹木幫助把沙子和土壤固定在一起且阻止它們被吹走。)

Ben: People are beginning to realize the importance of protecting the environment, aren't they? (班：人們開始領悟到保護環境的重要，不是嗎？)

Emma: Yes, I think so. (艾瑪：對，我也這樣想。)

Ben: When I was in China, it was very hot. Did you take lots of bottled water with you?

(班：當我在中國，天氣很熱。妳有隨身帶很多瓶裝水嗎？)

Emma: Yes, but we ran out once and had to drink water from a river.

(艾瑪：有，但是有一次我們用完了而必須喝河裡的水。)

Ben: That could make you sick. Many lakes and rivers are polluted by chemicals or dead animals. (班：那可能讓妳生病。很多湖泊和河流都被化學藥品或動物死屍污染了。)

Emma: I know, but we were very thirsty. Also, people are trying hard to make the water clean and the government is taking many measures to stop water pollution. The water in the lakes and rivers looked clean.

(艾瑪：我知道，但是我們很渴。而且，人們很努力試著淨化水質，政府也採取很多措施來阻止水污染。湖泊和河流中的水看起來是乾淨的。)

Ben: Even if the water looks clean, it could still be dirty, so you should always drink bottled water to be safe. (班：即使水看起來乾淨，它仍然可能是髒的，所以妳應該總是飲用瓶裝水以保安全。)

Emma: I see. (艾瑪：我懂了。)

● Emma and her friends travelled around China by __24.bus__ and sometimes by __25__.
(艾瑪和她的朋友在中國搭巴士有時候搭火車四處旅行。)

● Ben and his parents were caught in a sandstorm five years ago in Beijing and it was difficult to breathe and the sand even __26__ people.
(班和他的父母五年前在北京遇到一場沙塵暴，呼吸困難且沙子甚至傷害了人們。)

● Emma found that there were __27__ sandstorms in Beijing this time because people in Beijing are __28__ more trees.
(艾瑪發現這次北京有較少沙塵暴因為北京的人們正種植更多樹木。)

● Ben told Emma that it was dangerous to drink water from the river because some rivers and lakes were polluted by __29__ or dead animals.

(班告訴艾瑪喝河流裡的水是危險的因為有些河流和湖泊被化學藥品或動物死屍污染。)

● It would be __30__ for them to drink bottled water.

(喝瓶裝水對她們來說會是安全的。)

24. 答案：bus (巴士)
25. 答案：train (火車)
26. 答案：hurt (傷害)
27. 答案：fewer (更少)
28. 答案：planting (種植)
29. 答案：chemicals (化學藥品)
30. 答案：safe (安全)

夏朵英文

國中全新英語聽力測驗原文及參考答案

Unit 14

Ⅰ、Listen and choose the right picture.

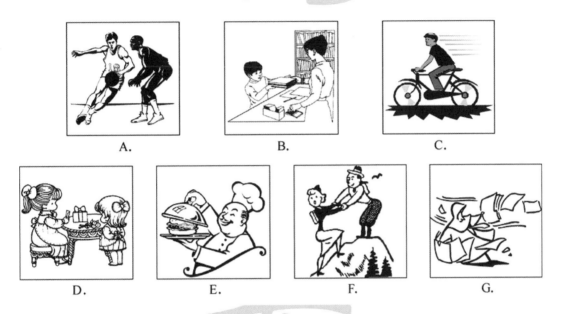

A.　　　　　B.　　　　　C.

D.　　　　E.　　　　F.　　　　G.

1. Hey, my dear. We finally reached the top of the mountain. What a nice view we have here!
   (嘿，親愛的。我們終於到達山頂了。這裡的風景真棒！)
   答案：(F)

2. Here's a card and my present for you, Jane. I hope you will like it.
   (這是一張卡片和我給妳的禮物，珍。我希望妳會喜歡它。)
   答案：(D)

3. Miss, may I take these two books home? (小姐，我可以把這兩本書帶回家嗎？)
   答案：(B)

4. My grandfather used to be a cook at the Park Hotel. (我祖父曾經是公園飯店的廚師。)
   答案：(E)

5. What a terrible day! I even can't walk in the wind. (多麼糟的天氣！在風中我甚至走不動。)
   答案：(G)

6. What's your plan for Sunday, Tom? How about having a basketball match with the students from Class 3?
   (你星期天的計劃是什麼，湯姆？和三班的學生們打一場籃球賽如何？)
   答案：(A)

7.   W: Shall we meet at the school gate at 2.00 in the afternoon?
     (女：我們要不要下午兩點在學校大門口碰面？)

     M: Sorry, I might be late. My piano lesson won't be over till 2.30. Can we meet at 3.00 in the afternoon? (男：抱歉，我可能會遲到。我的鋼琴課直到兩點半才會結束。我們可以下午三點碰面嗎？)

     W: No problem. See you then. (女：沒問題。到時候見。)

     Question: What time are they going to meet at the school gate?

     (問題：他們將幾點在學校大門碰面？)

     (A)At 2.00.   (B)At 2.30.   (C)At 3.00.   (D)At 3.30.
     答案：(C)

8.   M: Can I help you, Miss? (男：我可以效勞嗎，小姐？)

     W: Well, I'm looking for some CDs for my daughter. She likes S.H.E. best.
        (女：好，我正在為我女兒找一些 CD。她最喜歡 S.H.E.)

     M: How about this one? It's the latest. (男：這張怎麼樣？它是最新的。)

     W: OK. How much is it? (女：好。它多少錢？)

     M: 58 yuan. (男：五十八元。)

     Question: Where does this dialogue probably take place?

     (問題：這段對話可能發生在什麼場所？)

     (A)In a library. (在圖書館)   (B)In a CD shop. (在唱片行)
     (C)In a theater. (在電影院)   (D)In a restaurant. (在餐廳)
     答案：(B)

9.   W: How do you usually go to school, Mike? (女：你通常怎麼去學校，麥克？)

     M: I usually ride a bicycle. But if it rains, I go by bus.
        (男：我通常騎腳踏車。但如果下雨，我就搭巴士。)

     Question: How does Mike usually go to school? (問題：麥克通常怎麼去學校？)

     (A)By bus. (搭公車)   (B)By bike. (騎單車)   (C)On foot. (步行)   (D)By car. (開車)
     答案：(B)

10. W: Would you like to visit Alice with me after school? She's been ill for two days.
        (女：你想要放學後和我一起去拜訪艾莉絲嗎？她生病兩天了。)

     M: I'm afraid I can't. I have to take care of Mary, my little sister.
        (男：我恐怕不行。我必須照顧瑪莉，我妹妹。)

     W: That's OK. (女：沒關係。)

     Question: Why can't the boy visit Alice with the girl?

     (問題：為什麼這位男孩不能和這位女孩去拜訪艾莉絲？)

     (A)Because he has to look after his sister. (因為他要照顧妹妹。)

     (B)Because he will visit Mary. (因為他要去看 Mary。)

(C)Because he has visited Alice. (因為他已經去看過 Alice 了。)

(D)Because she will visit her. (因為她要去看她)

答案：(A)

11. W: What's in your big bag? (女：你的大袋子裡有什麼？)

M: Some food, drinks, a raincoat and some medicine.

(男：一些食物、飲料、一件雨衣和一些藥品。)

W: Have you got a camera and enough films? (女：你有一台相機和足夠的底片嗎？)

M: Sure. I like taking photos during my trip. (男：當然。我喜歡在我的旅途中拍照。)

Question: What's the boy going to do? (問題：這位男孩要去做什麼？)

(A)To have a picnic. (去野餐)　　　　　　(B)To take some films. (拍一些影片)

(C)To go on a trip. (去旅行)　　　　　　(D)To buy some food. (去買食物)

答案：(C)

12. M: Do you like the dishes here? Have you got any suggestions for us?

(男：妳喜歡這裡的料理嗎？妳有任何給我們的建議嗎？)

W: Well, the food is very delicious. I think I'll come here again.

(女：嗯，料理很美味。我想我會再次來這裡。)

Question: Who are the two speakers? (問題：這兩位對話者是誰？)

(A)Mum and son. (媽媽和兒子)　　　　　(B)Teacher and student. (老師和學生)

(C)Waiter and customer. (侍者和客人)　　(D)Host and guest. (主人和客人)

答案：(C)

13. W: What does your father do, John? (女：你父親的職業是什麼，約翰？)

M: He's a doctor, and my Mum is a nurse. They work in the same hospital. I hope I can be a doctor, too. (男：他是一名醫師，而我媽媽是一名護士。他們在同一間醫院工作。我希望我也可以成為一名醫師。)

W: That's very nice. I hope your dream will come true. (女：那很好。我希望你的夢想將成真。)

Question: What job does the boy's father do? (問題：這位男孩的父親是做什麼職業？)

(A)Dentist. (牙醫)　　(B)Nurse. (護士)　　(C)Teacher. (老師)　　(D)Doctor. (醫生)

答案：(D)

14. M: I've moved to my new flat at the seaside. (男：我搬去我在海邊的新公寓了。)

W: What's your new telephone number? (女：你的新電話號碼是幾號？)

M: 62580023. (男：62580023.)

W: That same as the old one? (女：那是和舊的一樣？)

M: No, my old telephone number was 64580023. (男：不，我的舊電話號碼是 64580023。)

Question: What's the boy's new telephone number? (問題：這位男孩的新電話號碼是？)

(A)64580023.　　　　(B)62580023.　　　　(C)64850023.　　　　(D)62850023.

答案：(B)

15. W: What do you usually have for breakfast on Sundays? (女：你星期天的早餐通常吃什麼？)

M: I usually have coffee and bread. What about you? (男：我通常喝咖啡吃麵包。那妳呢？)

W: I never have breakfast. So I often have a lot for lunch. I like beef and pork.

（女：我從來不吃早餐。所以我常常午餐吃很多。我喜歡牛肉和豬肉。）

Question: What does the woman usually have for breakfast?

(問題：這位女士通常早餐吃什麼？)

(A)Coffee and bread. (咖啡和麵包)   (B)Beef and pork. (牛肉和豬肉)

(C)Meat. (肉類)   (D)Nothing. (不吃早餐)

答案：(D)

16. W: Can I speak to Tom? (女：我可以和湯姆說話嗎？)

M: This is Tom speaking. (男：我就是湯姆。)

W: Well, this is Jenny. I bought a new computer this morning, but it doesn't work. I wonder if you can come and have a look. (女：喔，我是珍妮。我今天早上買了一台新電腦，但是它不能運作。我不知道你是否可以來看看。)

Question: Where are they talking? (問題：他們在哪裡對話？)

(A)On the phone. (在電話上)   (B)At Jenny's home. (在 Jenny 家)

(C)At the computer room. (在電腦室)   (D)At Tom's home. (在 Tom 家)

答案：(A)

Ⅲ、Listen to the passage and decide whether the following statements are True (T) or False (F).

I have several questions for you: Do you often see a blue sky above our city? Is the air in our city fresh? Is the water in our river clean? The answers to these questions are all "No"!

我有幾個問題要問你們：你們經常在我們的都市上空看到藍天嗎？我們都市的空氣新鮮嗎？我們河流中的水乾淨嗎？這些問題的答案都是「不」！

My grandfather often tells many interesting stories about his childhood. At that time, the sky was blue, the air was fresh and the water was clean. When my grandfather and his friends played in the forest, they could hear birds sing. When they swam in the river, they could see many fish. It was a happy time.

我的祖父經常講很多關於他童年的有趣故事。在那時候，天空是藍的，空氣是新鮮的而且水是乾淨的。當我的祖父和他的朋友們在森林裡玩，他們可以聽到鳥兒在唱歌。當他們在河中游泳，他們可以看到很多魚。那是個快樂的時光。

However, today, the air and water are becoming dirtier. People are killing animals, and cutting down and burning trees. Some animals and plants are now disappearing. The earth is in trouble.

然而，今天，空氣和水變得比較髒。人們殘殺動物，還砍伐且焚燒樹木。有些動物和植物現在正在消失中。這地球陷入麻煩了。

I want you to join us by helping protect our environment. We need to protect Earth because it is our home. We do not need to do big things — we can start out small. Do not throw any rubbish onto the ground. Do not waste water. Use both sides of paper when you write. Stop using plastic bags for shopping.

我希望你們加入我們一起幫助保護我們的環境。我們需要保護地球因為它是我們的家。我們不需要做大不了的事 — 我們可以從小處著手。不要把任何垃圾丟到地上。不要浪費水。當你書寫時使用紙的兩面。停止使用塑膠袋購物。

This is our world. Let's do our best to make it more beautiful.

這是我們的世界。讓我們盡力使它更美麗。

17. The speakers asked three questions at the beginning and the answers to these questions are all "No".(講者在一開始問了三個問題而這些問題的答案都是「不」。)
答案：(T 對)

18. Grandmother often tells the speaker some stories about her childho
(祖母經常講一些關於她童年的故事給講者聽。)
答案：(F 錯)

19. It seems that in the city people lived in a cleaner environment many years ago.
(看樣子在都市的人們多年前住在一個較乾淨的環境。)
答案：(T 對)

20. The speaker told us that people are doing something bad to the city now.
(講者告訴我們人們現在正在對都市做一些有害的事。)
答案：(T 對)

21. The speaker thought that the Earth is in trouble.(講者認為地球正陷入麻煩。)
答案：(T對)

22. The speaker seemed to be a member of an organization which helps protect the environment.
(講者似乎是一個幫助保護環境的組織的成員。)
答案：(T 對)

23. The speaker suggested we reuse plastic bags for shopping.
(講者建議我們重複使用購物塑膠袋。)
答案：(F 錯)

IV、Listen to the dialogue and fill in the blanks.

Ben: Hi, Angela, I am writing an article, "How do you feel about these problems?", for our school newspaper. Can you give me a hand?
(班：嗨，安吉拉，我正在為我們的校刊寫一篇文章,「你對這些問題感覺如何？」妳可以幫我個忙嗎？)

Angela: No problem. (安吉拉：沒問題。)

Ben: First, I will tell you about a problem. Then I will ask you, "How do you feel about it?" There are three choices for your answer: not worried at all, a little worried or very worried. OK?
(班：首先，我將告訴妳一個問題。然後我會問妳，妳對此感覺如何？妳有三個選項可以回答：完全不擔憂，有點擔憂，或是很擔憂。好嗎？)

Angela: OK. (安吉拉：好。)

Ben: Here's the first problem: People throwing rubbish in parks, streets and other places. How do you feel about it? (班：這是第一個問題：人們在公園街到和其他地方丟垃圾。妳對此感覺如何？)

Angela: Oh, those people don't care about the environment or about other people. That's so bad. My answer is "very worried". (安吉拉：噢，這些人不在乎環境或其他人。真糟糕。我的答案是「很擔憂」。)

Ben: Now, the second one: People making a lot of noise. (班：現在，第二個：人們製造很多噪音。)

Angela: I'm not worried about this. We can put something over our ears. My answer is "not worried at all".(安吉拉：我不為此擔憂。我們可以用某種東西蓋住耳朵。我的答案是「完全不擔憂」。)

Ben: Got it. Now, the third one: People polluting the water and the air.

(班：明白了。現在，第三個：人們污染水和空氣。)

Angela: Well, no one can live without water or air. My answer is "very worried".

(安吉拉：嗯，沒有人可以在沒有水或空氣之下生活。我的答案是「很擔憂」。)

Ben: That's what I think too. The last problem: A lot of traffic on the road.

(班：我也是那樣想。最後一個問題：道路交通擁擠。)

Angela: Well, my answer is "a little worried". (安吉拉：嗯，我的答案是「有點擔憂」。)

Ben: Well, that's all. Thanks a lot. (班：好，就這些。多謝了。)

Angela: My pleasure.　(安吉拉：我很樂意。)

QUESTIONNAIRE: How do you feel about these __24__?

(問卷：你對這些問題有什麼感覺？)

Your choices: (你的選項)

A＞not worried at all　完全不擔憂

B＞a __25__ worried　有點擔憂

C＞very worried　很擔憂

Question 1: People throwing __26__ in parks, streets and __27__ places.

(問題一：人們在公園街到和其他地方丟垃圾。)

Question 2: People making a lot of __28__. (問題二：人們製造很多噪音。)

Question 3: People __29__ the water and the air. (問題三：人們污染水和空氣。)

Question 4: A lot of __30__ on the road. (問題四：道路交通擁擠。)

24. 答案：problems

25. 答案：little

26. 答案：rubbish

27. 答案：other

28. 答案：noise

29. 答案：polluting

30. 答案：traffic

夏朵英文

國中全新英語聽力測驗原文及參考答案

Unit 15

Ⅰ、Listen and choose the right picture.

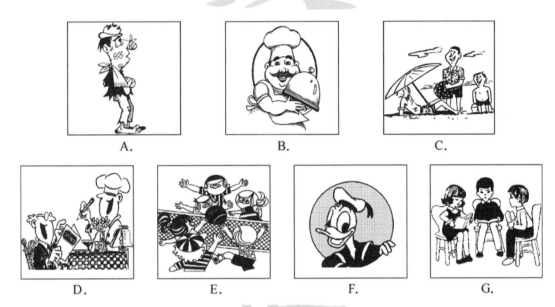

A.   B.   C.

D.   E.   F.   G.

1. Can't you see the ball's coming? Hey! Stop them, Peter!
   (你看不到球正飛過來嗎？嘿！阻止他們，彼得！)
   答案：(E)

2. Donald Duck is one of the most popular characters in Walt Disney's cartoons.
   (唐老鴨是華德迪士尼的卡通中最受歡迎的角色之一。)
   答案：(F)

3. Don't lie under the umbrella! Put on your swimming suit and let's go to the sea.
   (不要躺在傘下！穿上妳的泳裝一起到海裡去吧。)
   答案：(C)

4. Sir, may I have your order now? (先生，我現在可以為您點餐了嗎？)
   答案：(D)

5. What's the matter with you, Billy? Was there an accident just now?
   (你是怎麼了，比利？剛才是不是發生了一場意外？)
   答案：(A)

6. Do you know this word, Ben and Mary? You can look it up in your book!
   (班和瑪莉，你們認識這個字嗎？你們可以在你們的書裡查查它。)
   答案：(G)

7.　W: What time shall we start for Shanghai International Financial Centre?
　　　（女：我們應該幾點出發去上海國際金融中心？）

　　M: How about a quarter to eight?（男：七點四十五分如何？）

　　W: No, let's make it thirty-five minutes later because it is not very far from here.
　　　（女：不，讓我們晚個三十五分鐘因為它距離這邊不很遠。）

　　Question: When will they start for Shanghai International Financial Centre?
　　（問題：他們幾點會出發去上海國際金融中心？）

　　(A)7.45.　　　　　　(B)8.20.　　　　　　(C)8.15.　　　　　　(D)8.25.
　　答案：(B)

8.　M: Hello, may I speak to May?（男：哈囉，我可以和玫講話嗎？）

　　W: Sorry. She has gone to the library. Can I take a message for her?
　　　（女：抱歉。她去圖書館了。我可以幫您留話給她嗎？）

　　M: Thank you. This is Jack. Please tell her that I have changed my phone number. It used to be 56940213. But now it is 56639304.（男：謝謝。我是傑克。請告訴她我更改了我的電話號碼。本來是 56940213。但現在是 56639304。）

　　Question: What is Jack's telephone number now?（問題：傑克現在的電話號碼是？）

　　(A)56940213.　　　　(B)56942310.　　　　(C)56639304.　　　　(D)56693304.
　　答案：(C)

9.　W: Good evening, sir. What can I do for you?（女：晚安，先生。我能為您做什麼？）

　　M: Good evening. My name is Steven. I have booked a room here.
　　　（男：晚安。我名叫史蒂芬。我在這裡預定了一個房間。）

　　W: Let me see. Oh, yes. Your room is Room 5018. Your ID card, please!
　　　（女：讓我看看。喔，對。您的房間是 5018 號房。請借我您的身分證！）

　　Question: Where are they talking now?（問題：他們現在在哪裡對話？）

　　(A)At the reception desk.(在接待櫃台)

　　(B)In Room 5018. (在 5018 房內)

　　(C)In a restaurant. (在餐廳)

　　(D)In a bookshop. (在書店)

　　答案：(A)

10.　M: My brother will get to Shanghai in two hours. How shall we go to the airport?
　　　（男：我兄弟將在兩小時內到上海。我們該怎麼去機場？）

　　W: Shall we go there by underground or by bus?（女：我們應該搭地鐵或搭巴士去？）

　　M: Neither. It will take us a lot of time. I think we'd better take a taxi instead of the underground or a bus.（男：都不好。那將會花很多時間。我想我們最好搭計程車而非地鐵或巴士。）

　　W: OK.（女：好。）

Question: How will they get to the airport? (問題：他們將如何去機場？)

(A)By train.(搭火車)   (B)By bus. (搭巴士)

(C)By underground. (搭地鐵)   (D)By taxi. (搭計程車)

答案：(D)

11. M: Would you like to go to the cinema with me this afternoon?

(男：妳今天下午想跟我去看電影嗎？)

W: I'd love to, but my mother will come back from Canada this afternoon, so I have to meet her at the airport and we will have a big meal tonight.

(女：我很想去，但是我母親今天下午將從加拿大回來，所以我必須去機場接她然後我們今晚將吃頓大餐。)

M: May I go with you? I haven't seen your mother for a long time.

(男：我可以跟妳一起去嗎？我很久沒見到妳母親了。)

W: That's great. (女：那太好了。)

Question: What will the man do this afternoon? (問題：這位男士今天下午將做什麼？)

(A)Go to the cinema. (去看電影)   (B)Have a big meal. (吃大餐)

(C)Stay at home. (待在家)   (D)Go to the airport. (去機場)

答案：(D)

12. W: May I take your order now? (女：我現在可以為您點餐了嗎？)

M: Yes. I think we are ready to order. (男：好的。我想我們準備好點餐了。)

W: What would you like? (女：您想吃什麼？)

Question: Where does this conversation probably take place?

(問題：這段對話可能是在哪裡發生？)

(A)At a restaurant. (在餐廳。)   (B)In a hotel. (在旅館)

(C)In a supermarket. (在超市)   (D)At the cinema. (在電影院)

答案：(A)

13. W: Well, Mr White, I've completed my examination and there is nothing serious with your baby.

(女：嗯，懷特先生，我已完成了我的檢查而您的嬰兒沒有什麼嚴重問題。)

M: Don't you think she should take an X-ray? (男：妳不認為她應該照個X光嗎？)

Question: What job does the woman do? (問題：這位女士是做什麼職業的？)

(A)A dentist. (牙醫)   (B)A doctor. (醫師。)   (C)A teacher. (老師)   (D)A trainer. (訓練員)

答案：(B)

14. W: You speak English very fluently. (女：你英語說得很流利。)

M: Thank you. (男：謝謝。)

W: How long have you learned English?(女：你學英文多久了？)

M: I've learned English since twelve years ago. My mother began to teach me when I was four years old. (男：我從十二年前開始學英文。我母親在我四歲的時候開始教我。)

Question: How old is the man? (問題：這位男士幾歲？)

(A)12 years old.   (B)14 years old.   (C)15 years old.   (D)16 years old.

答案：(D)

15. W: My dog doesn't seem to be as friendly as yours. (女：我的狗似乎不像你的那麼友善。)

M: I don't think so. Yours is much friendlier than mine.

(男：我不這樣認為。妳的比我的友善多了。)

Question: What does the woman think of the man's dog?

(問題：這位女士認為這位男士的狗如何？)

(A)Friendlier. (比較友善。)

(B)Not friendly. (不友善)

(C)Not as friendly as hers. (不像她的狗那麼友善)

(D)As friendly as hers. (跟她的狗一樣友善)

答案：(A)

16. W: Why did your father hurry off yesterday? (女：為何你的父親昨天匆忙離開？)

M: He was afraid that he would miss the plane. (男：他恐怕他會錯過班機。)

Question: Why did the boy's father hurry off? (問題：為何這位男孩的父親匆忙離開？)

(A)He got up late this morning. (他今天晚起床。)

(B)He hurried off to catch a plane. (他匆忙離開去趕飛機。)

(C)He was afraid that he would be late for the train. (他怕趕不上火車。)

(D)He hurried off to catch a train. (他匆忙去趕火車。)

答案：(B)

Ⅲ、Listen to the passage and decide whether the following statements are True (T) or False (F).

Good afternoon, and welcome to England. We hope that your visit will be a pleasant one. Today, I would like to draw your attention to a few of our laws.

午安，歡迎到英國。我希望你們的旅程將是愉快的。今天，我想請大家注意我們的幾條法令。

The first one is about drinking. Now, you may not buy wine in this country if you are under 18 years old. Neither may your friends. They may not buy it for you.

第一條是關於飲酒。現在，在這個國家你如果低於十八歲就不能購買酒。你的朋友們也不行。他們不能幫你買。

Secondly, noise. Enjoy yourself as you like, but please don't make unnecessary noise, especially at night. We ask you to show your friendliness to others who may wish to be quiet.

第二，噪音。你可以隨意享受，但是請不要製造不必要的噪音，特別是在晚上。我們要求你對那些可能希望你安靜的其他人表示出你的友善。

Thirdly, crossing the road. Be careful. The traffic moves on the left side of the road in this country. Use the pedestrian crossing and take great care when crossing the road.

第三，過馬路。要小心。在這個國家交通靠馬路的左邊前進。使用人行穿越道並且在過馬路時加緊小心。

My next point is about litter. It is against the law to drop litter in the street. When you have something to throw away, please put it in your pocket and take it home, or put it in a litter bin. Finally it is also against the law to buy cigarettes if you are under 16 years of age.

我的下一個重點是關於垃圾。在街道上丟垃圾是違反法律的。當你有些東西要丟棄，請將它放在你的口袋並帶回家，或將它放到垃圾桶。最後如果你的年齡低於十六歲購買香菸也是違法的。

I'd like to finish by saying that if you need any sort of help or assistance, you should get in touch with your local police station. They will be very pleased to help you.

我想以此作為結語：如果你需要任何方面的幫忙或協助，你應該連絡你當地的警察局。他們會很樂意幫助你。

Now, are there any questions?

現在，有任何問題嗎？

17. According to the passage, the listeners might be the people in the city.
    (根據此短文，聽眾們可能是本市的人們。)
    答案：(F 錯)

18. In this country, if you are under 18 years of age, you may not buy wine, but your friend can buy it for you.
    (在這個國家，如果你年齡低於十八歲，你不能買酒，但是你的朋友們可以幫你買。)
    答案：(F 錯)

19. The speaker told the listeners not to make unnecessary noise at night. But they can in the day time. (講者告訴聽眾們晚上不要製造不必要的噪音。但是他們在白天可以。)
    答案：(F 錯)

20. It's important for the listeners to cross the streets by using the pedestrian crossings in England.
    (在英國過馬路時使用人行穿越道對聽眾們來說是很重要的。)
    答案：(T 對)

21. You may buy cigarettes if you are above 16 years of age.
    (如果你年齡超過十六歲你就可以購買香菸。)
    答案：(T 對)

22. It is against the law to put the litter in your pocket and take it home.
    (把垃圾放在你的口袋並且帶回家是違反法律的。)
    答案：(F 錯)

23. A policeman probably makes the speech. (或許是一位警察在演講。)
    答案：(T 對)

Simon: Welcome to the programme. Today, Auntie Wang is here with us to answer your questions. Your first question is about blind people. Auntie Wang, can blind people hear better than other people?

賽門：歡迎加入課程。今天，王阿姨來到我們當中來回答你們的問題。你們的第一個問題是關於盲人。王阿姨，盲人比其他人聽得更清楚嗎？

Wang: No. Good listening skills are very useful for blind people, but they don't hear better than other people. They just use their hearing more than people with sight.

王：不。好的聆聽技巧對盲人來說很有用，但他們並不比其他人聽得更清楚。他們只是比看得到的人更常運用他們的聽覺。

Simon: What about deaf people? Can deaf people do things more easily than blind people?

賽門：聽障人士如何？聽障人士比盲人做起事情來要容易嗎？

Wang: Yes. Deaf people can do most things without any help, while blind people often need help when they go to new places or do new things.

王：是的。聽障人士可在不用幫忙之下做大部分事情，然而當去到新的場所或做新的事情時盲人經常需要幫助。

Simon: Many listeners asked, "Why can't many deaf people speak?" Can you explain that, Auntie Wang?

賽門：很多聽眾問到，「為何很多聽障人士不能講話？」您可以解釋一下嗎，王阿姨？

Wang: Yes, of course. The reason is quite simple. When people learn to speak, they listen first, and then speak. Some deaf people are not able to speak because they never get the chance to hear the language.

王：好，當然。原因頗簡單。當人們學習講話，他們先聽，然後講話。有些聽障人士無法講話因為他們從來沒有機會聽到這個語言。

Simon: How do they communicate then?

賽門：那麼他們如何溝通呢？

Wang: They usually use sign language to "talk".

王：他們通常使用手語來「講話」。

Simon: Interesting. Well, now all of our listeners know more about blind and deaf people. Auntie Wang, thank you for coming today.

賽門：真有趣。好，現在我們全體聽眾對盲人和聽障人士有更多了解了。王阿姨，謝謝您今天過來。

Wang: It was a pleasure.

王：樂意之至。

For blind people(關於盲人)

- good __24__ skills are useful for them (好的聆聽技巧對他們來說很有用)
- they __25__ hear better than other people (他們不比其他人聽得更清楚)
- they use their hearing __26__ than people with __27__
  (他們比看得到的人更常用他們的聽覺)

For deaf people(關於聽障人士)
- they do things more __28__ than blind people (他們比盲人做事情更容易)
- they never get the __29__ to hear the language (他們從來沒有機會聽到這個語言)
- they use __30__ language to communicate (他們使用手語來溝通)

24. 答案：listening
25. 答案：don't
26. 答案：more
27. 答案：sight
28. 答案：easily
29. 答案：chance
30. 答案：sign

夏朵英文

國中全新英語聽力測驗原文及參考答案

Unit 16

Ⅰ、Listen and choose the right picture.

1. Why did you leave the fan on in your room? It's a waste of electricity!
   (你為何離開房間沒有關電扇？這樣很浪費電！)
   答案：(A)

2. What a smell! What's wrong with the steak? Oh, it's burnt.
   (什麼怪味！牛排怎麼了？喔，它燒焦了。)
   答案：(C)

3. Taking photos is not allowed on Philip Island. It may hurt these little penguins' eyes.
   (在飛利浦島上不准許拍照。它可能傷害到這些小企鵝的眼睛。)
   答案：(E)

4. Bob, stop! You should ride your bicycle in the playground!
   (包博，停住！你應該在操場騎你的腳踏車！)
   答案：(F)

5. A man was knocked down by a fast car on Sunshine Road yesterday.
   (一位男士昨天在陽光路被一輛快速的車撞倒了。)
   答案：(B)

6. Why is Cathy chasing Benny? Are they playing a game?
   (凱西為何在追逐班妮？她們在玩遊戲嗎？)
   答案：(D)

7.　W: Where are you leaving, Mark? (女：你要出發去哪裡，馬克？)

M: I'm leaving for Boston. (男：我要出發去波士頓。)

W: Who are you going to see? (女：你要去看誰？)

M: I'm going to see my grandparents. You know, they feel lonely because my parents and I don't live with them. I often go there once a half year.

(男：我要去看我的祖父母。妳知道的，他們感到寂寞因為我父母和我不和他們住在一起。我通常半年去那裡一次。)

Question: How often does Mark go to see his grandparents?

問題：馬克多久去拜訪他的祖父母？

(A)Once a year. (一年一次)　　　　　　　　(B)Twice a month. (一個月兩次)

(C)Twice a year. (一年兩次。)　　　　　　　(D)Twice a half year. (半年兩次)

答案：(C)

8.　W: Haven't you finished reading the book yet? (女：你還沒讀完那本書嗎？)

M: No. I'm busy preparing for the test these days. I still have one third left.

(男：還沒。我最近幾天忙著準備考試。我還剩三分之一。)

W: That is to say, you'll have to read 200 pages before next Tuesday.

(女：那就是說，你下星期二之前必須讀兩百頁。)

Question: How many pages has the boy read? (問題：這位男孩已經讀了多少頁？)

(A)200.　　　　　(B)300.　　　　　(C)400.　　　　　(D)600.

答案：(C)

9.　W: Watch out! You can't dive here. (女：小心！你不能在這裡跳水。)

M: Why? I am not poor at swimming. The swimming pool is used for swimming and diving.

(男：為什麼？我會游泳。游泳池是用來游泳和跳水的。)

W: That's dangerous! Look, there is no water in it. (女：那樣很危險！你看，裡面沒有水。)

Question: Why can't the man dive? (問題：這位男士為何不能跳水？)

(A)There is not any water. (那裡根本沒有水。)

(B)He is not so good at swimming. (他並不很擅長游泳。)

(C)He should watch out before diving. (他跳水前要小心。)

(D)All of the answers are right. (答案都對。)

答案：(A)

10. M: Excuse me, would you like to spare me a few minutes?

(男：不好意思，您可以抽幾分鐘給我嗎？)

W: Yes, if it is not too long. (女：好，只要不是太久。)

M: I hate being lost. Can you tell me the way to City Park?

(男：我討厭迷路。您可以告訴我怎麼去城市公園嗎？)

W: Let me see. You may first take a minibus at the street corner and get off at Wood Road. Then you may change to No.928 bus at the same bus stop. It will take you right there. You can't miss it.(女：我看看。你可以先在街角搭迷你巴士在伍德路下車。然後你可以在同一個公車站轉搭 928 號巴士。它會帶你直達那裡。你不會錯過的。)

M: Thank you so much. (男：多謝您喔。)

Question: How many buses should the man take? (問題：這位男士應該搭幾趟巴士？)

(A)One. (一趟)　　　　(B)Two. (兩趟)　　　　(C)Three. (三趟)　　　　(D)Four. (四趟)

答案：(B)

11. W: What can I do for you, sir? (女：我能為您效勞嗎，先生？)

M: Yes, I'm looking for a sunhat for my mother. (男：是，我正在為我母親找一頂遮陽帽。)

W: How about this one? It's cheaper because this kind of sunhat is on sale this week.

(女：這一頂怎麼樣？它比較便宜因為這種遮陽帽本星期正在特價。)

M: The style and material are OK. But she will not like the colour.

(男：這款式和材質都可以。但是她不會喜歡這個顏色。)

Question: Why doesn't the man want to buy the sunhat?

(問題：為何這位男士不想買這頂遮陽帽？)

(A)Because sunhats are getting cheaper and cheaper. (因為遮陽帽愈來愈便宜。)

(B)Because he is not able to pay for it. (因為他買不起。)

(C)Because his mother is not with him. (因為他媽媽不在身邊。)

(D)Because his mother doesn't like the color. (因為他母親不喜歡這個顏色。)

答案：(D)

12. W: Why are you so late, Steve? (女：你為何遲到那麼久，史蒂夫？)

M: There is something wrong with my watch and it walks slowly.

(男：我的手錶有點毛病它走得慢。)

Question: Why is Steve late? (問題：史蒂夫為何遲到？)

(A)Because he lost his watch. (因為他的手錶丟了。)

(B)Because his watch is too fast. (因為他的手錶太快。)

(C)Because his watch is too slow. (因為他的手錶太慢。)

(D)Because his watch doesn't work. (因為他的手錶停了。)

答案：(C)

13. W: Hi, that pair of goggles looks nice. How much does it cost?

(女：嗨，那副蛙鏡看起來很棒。它多少錢？)

M: One hundred and eighty yuan. (男：一百八十元。)

W: Oh! That's too dear. But I want to take it. (女：噢！太貴了吧。但我想要買。)

Question: The lady will buy the goggles, won't she?

(問題：那位婦女將會買那副蛙鏡，對吧？)

(A)Yes, she did. (是的，她買了。)　　　　(B)Yes, she will. (是的，她會買。)

(C)No, she didn't. (不，她沒買。)　　　　(D)No, she won't. (不，她不要買。)

答案：(B)

14. W: What's the matter with you? You look so pale. (女：你是怎麼回事？你看來好蒼白。)

M: I had lunch at the noodle stall at the school gate. Now I have some pain in my stomach.

(男：我在校門口的麵攤吃了午餐。現在我有些胃痛。)

W: Shall I ask the doctor in the school clinic to help you?

(女：我應該請學校保健室的醫師幫助你嗎？)

M: That's very kind of you. (男：妳真好心。)

Question: Where will the girl go? (問題：這位女孩將去哪裡？)

(A)To the hospital. (去醫院)   (B)To his home. (回家)

(C)To the school clinic. (去學校保健室)   (D)To the school gate. (去學校大門)

答案：(C)

15. W: What are you doing, Arthur? (女：你在幹嘛，亞瑟？)

M: I'm publishing a class newspaper. (男：我正在出版一份班報。)

W: Oh, how beautifully you are drawing! (女：喔，你畫得好美唷！)

M: It's kind of you to say so. (男：妳真好心這樣誇我。)

Question: How are the pictures in the class newspaper? (問題：班報裡的圖畫如何？)

(A)Not bad. (不賴)   (B)Well. (不錯)   (C)Beautifully. (美麗地)(D)Wonderful. (很讚。)

答案：(D)

16. W: What time did you get to Ocean Park? (女：你幾點到海洋公園的？)

M: At 10.30 a.m. (男：上午十點三十分。)

W: Did you meet Nancy there? (女：你有在那邊見到南西嗎？)

M: Yes, of course. She had waited for half an hour before I arrived.

(男：有啊，當然。在我到達之前她等了半小時。)

Question: What time did Nancy get there? (問題：南西是幾點到達的？)

(A)9.30.   (B)8.30.   (C)10.00.   (D)10.30.

答案：(C)

Ⅲ、Listen to the passage and decide whether the following statements are True (T) or False (F).

Television pictures fool your eyes. When you look at a picture, your brain holds the picture for one-tenth of a second, then you must look again. So when the brain has to hold more than ten pictures a second, it puts them together as moving pictures. You can see this yourself by drawing a lot of pictures of the same person, one on each page of a notebook. Then turn the pages of the notebook very quickly. The person will seem to move.

電視畫面會愚弄你的眼睛。當你看一個畫面時，你的腦將此畫面抓住十分之一秒，然後你必須再看一次。所以當腦每秒必須抓住超過十個畫面時，它將它們放在一起成為動畫。你可以透過在一本筆記本畫很多同一個人的圖樣，一頁一幅來自己測試。畫好後將筆記本快速翻頁。這個人會好像在動。

A television picture uses a series of lines across the screen. The lines change the picture many times each second and make moving pictures. We call this kind of television "analogue television".

電視畫面運用一系列線條跨越螢幕。這些線條每秒改變畫面很多次製造出動態畫面。我們稱這種電視「類比電視」。

Now we have "digital television". It has no lines. Both sound and pictures are in numbers. When the numbers on a digital television change, only the differences between the old picture and the new one change. So the change is very fast and the picture and sound quality are very good.

現在我們有「數位電視」。它沒有線條。聲音和畫面兩者都是數據。當數位電視上的數據改變，只有舊畫面和新畫面的差異部分改變。所以這改變很快速而畫面和音效品質很好。

17. Our brains can hold a picture for one-tenth of a second.

(我們的腦可以抓住一個畫面十分之一秒。)

答案：(T 對)

18. If we want to form moving pictures in our minds, there needs to be at least twenty pictures a second.(如果我們想要在我們的腦中形成動畫，至少需要一秒二十張圖。)

答案：(F 錯)

19. We can make moving pictures on the notebook by ourselves according to the speaker.

(根據講者，我們可以自己在筆記本上製做出動畫。)

答案：(T 對)

20. Analogue televisions have sound and pictures in numbers.

(類比電視有數位化的音效和畫面。)

答案：(F 錯)

21. In fact, an analogue television changes pictures many times each second to make moving pictures. (事實上，一台類比電視每秒變更畫面很多次以製造出動畫。)

答案：(T 對)

22. A digital television doesn't change pictures as often as an analogue television.

(數位電視不像模擬電視變更畫面那麼頻繁。)

答案：(T 對)

23. According to the speaker, the picture and sound quality of an analogue television is much better.

(根據講者，類比電視的畫面和音效品質好得多。)

答案：(F 錯)

IV、Listen to the passage and fill in the blanks

Electricity is very useful in our daily life. It helps make our lives easier. A lot of things use electricity at our homes. Here are three of them, and advice on their use.

電在我們每天日常生活當中很有用。它幫助我們的生活更輕鬆。在我們的家中有很多東西使用電。這裡列出三種，以及它們使用上的建議。

Using different electricity appliances
使用不同的電器用具

Rice cookers (電鍋)

Using a rice cooker is simple and cheap. However, to use it safely, you should do the following：
使用電鍋是簡單又經濟的。然而，要安全地使用它，妳應該照下列方法：

- Keep the outside of the pot dry. (維持鍋外側乾燥。)
- Not leave the pot on when it is empty. (不要在空鍋時維持運作。)

Washing machines (洗衣機)

A washing machine can help people a lot. It frees office workers and housewives from washing clothes. However, it can be dangerous. You should be careful of the following：(洗衣機可幫人們很大忙。它讓上班族和家庭主婦不受洗衣服困擾。然而，它可能是危險的。你應該小心下列事項：)

- Do not put your hand in a washing machine when it is on. (不要把你的手放進運轉中的洗衣機。)
- Unplug it when you are not using it. (當沒有在使用時把插頭拔掉。)

Microwaves (微波爐)

A lot of people use a microwave at home. You can use it to heat water or cook food. However, to use a microwave safely, you should do the following：(很多人在家裡使用微波爐。你可以用它加熱水或烹調食物。然而，要安全地使用微波爐，你應該做下列事情：)

- Do not turn it on when it is empty, because it might start a fire.
  (當它是空的時候不要啟動，因為這可能釀成火災。)
- Stand 3 to 4 feet away from the microwave when it is on, just to be on the safe side.
  (當運轉時，站在距離微波爐三到四尺，純粹為了確保安全。)
- Before you use any glass or plastic containers in a microwave, make sure they are "microwave safe".
  (你在微波爐使用任何玻璃或塑膠容器之前，確認它們是「微波安全」的。)
- Do not use metal containers in the microwave.
  (不要在微波爐使用金屬容器。)

24. 答案：outside (外側)
25. 答案：empty (空的)
26. 答案：hand (手)
27. 答案：using (使用)
28. 答案：fire (火災)
29. 答案：4/four (四)
30. 答案：metal (金屬)

夏朵英文

國中全新英語聽力測驗原文及參考答案

Unit 17

I 、Listen and choose the right picture.

A.　　　　　　　　B.　　　　　　　　C.

D.　　　　　E.　　　　　F.　　　　　G.

1. It's a waste of water if you clean your face under a running tap.
   (如果你開著水龍頭洗臉很浪費水。)
   答案：(F)

2. Do you enjoy singing Karaoke in your spare time? (你在空閒時間喜歡唱卡拉 OK 嗎？)
   答案：(G)

3. Keep silent, Joe! It's the reading room, not your home.
   (保持安靜，喬！這是閱讀室，不是你家。)
   答案：(A)

4. Sorry, sir. No dogs are allowed here. So take your dog away!
   (抱歉，先生。這裡不允許狗進入。所以把你的狗帶開吧！)
   答案：(E)

5. A vet is someone who makes sick animals better. (獸醫是讓生病的動物好起來的人。)
   答案：(D)

6. I know that Kelvin keeps fit by swimming three times a week.
   (我知道凱文靠一星期游泳三次維持健康。)
   答案：(B)

7.　W: Can I help you? (女：我能為您效勞嗎？)

M: Yes, I'd like to buy a pair of goggles. Can you show me one?

(男：是的，我想買一副蛙鏡。妳可以拿一副給我看嗎？)

W: Sure. What about this black one? (女：當然。這副黑色的如何？)

M: It's OK. But it isn't as nice as that brown one. But that brown one is too expensive for me to buy. (男：還好。但是它沒有咖啡色那副那麼好。但是那副咖啡色的太貴我買不起。)

Question: Which pair of goggles will the man probably buy?

(問題：這位男士大概會買哪一副蛙鏡？)

(A)The pair of black goggles.(黑色蛙鏡)　　　(B)Neither. (都不買。)

(C)The pair of brown goggles.(咖啡色蛙鏡)　　(D)Either. (兩副都買)

答案：(B)

8.　W: What's wrong with you? You look very pale. (女：你怎麼了？你看起來很蒼白。)

M: I feel sick. Last night I stayed up too late to get up early this morning. So I hardly had any time to prepare breakfast, so I have had a stomachache. (男：我不舒服。昨晚我熬到太晚以致今天早上不能早起。所以我幾乎沒有任何時間準備早餐，所以我胃痛了。)

W: You'd better see the doctor. (女：你最好去看醫生。)

M: Yes, I will. Thank you. (男：對，我會去。謝謝。)

Question: Why did the man get up very late? (問題：為何這位男士很晚起床。)

(A)Because he had gone to bed too late the night before. (因為他前一晚太晚睡。)

(B)Because he felt ill. (因為他病了。)

(C)Because he had little time. (因為他沒時間。)

(D)Because he had a stomachache. (因為他胃痛。)

答案：(A)

9.　W: How will you get to the airport? (女：你將怎麼去機場？)

M: I have no idea. Taking a bus is much cheaper. I may go there on a bus.

(男：我不知道。搭巴士便宜很多。我可能會搭巴士去。)

W: You'd better not. Today is Sunday. Buses must be very crowded. You'd better call a taxi.

(女：你最好不要。今天是星期天。巴士可能會很擠。你最好叫計程車。)

M: I'll follow your advice. (男：我會遵照妳的建議。)

Question: How will the man get to the airport? (問題：這位男士將怎麼去機場？)

(A)By bike. (騎單車)　　　　　　　　(B)By subway. (搭地鐵)

(C)By taxi. (搭計程車)　　　　　　　(D)By bus. (坐巴士)

答案：(C)

10.　W: Excuse me. I'm looking for a bunch of bananas. (女：不好意思。我正在找一串香蕉。)

M: Sorry. There aren't any more bananas. We've sold out all of them.

(男：抱歉。已經沒有任何香蕉了。我們全都賣完了。)

W: There aren't? (女：沒有嗎？)

M: No, there aren't. Sorry. (男：對，沒有了。抱歉。)

Question: Where does the conversation probably take place?

(問題：這段對話可能是在哪裡發生？)

(A)In the street. (在街上)　　　　　　　(B)In a fruit shop. (在一間水果店)

(C)In a flower shop. (在水果店)　　　　(D)At a restaurant. (在餐廳)

答案：(B)

11. W: I went to watch an exciting match instead of staying at home yesterday afternoon. What about you? (女：昨天下午我去看了一場精彩的球賽而沒有待在家裡。那你呢？)

M: My friend asked me to go fishing with him. But I went shopping with my wife.

(男：我朋友邀我和他一起去釣魚。但是我和我太太一起去購物了。)

Question: What did the woman do yesterday afternoon?

(問題：這位女士昨天下午做了什麼？)

(A)She stayed at home. (她待在家裡。)　　(B)She went shopping. (她去購物。)

(C)She went fishing. (她去釣魚。)　　　　(D)She watched a match. (她看了一場球賽。)

答案：(D)

12. W: May I use your dictionary, Mike? (女：我可以用你的字典嗎，麥克？)

M: Sorry. It was on the desk. But I have just lent it to Rita. She has gone back home.

(男：抱歉。它本來在書桌上。但是我剛剛才把它借給瑞塔了。她回家去了。)

Question: Where is the dictionary? (問題：字典在哪裡？)

(A)At Mike's home. (在麥克家)　　　　(B)At Rita's home. (在瑞塔家)

(C)On the desk. (在桌上)　　　　　　(D)At the school. (在學校)

答案：(B)

13. W: How long have you been away from your hometown? (女：你離開你家鄉多久了？)

M: For thirty-five years. I've been away from there since I was twenty.

(男：三十五年。我自從二十歲起就沒在那邊。)

Question: How old is the man? (問題：這位男士幾歲？)

(A)30 years old. (30 歲)　　　　　　　(B)35 years old. (35 歲)

(C)20 years old. (20 歲)　　　　　　　(D)55 years old. (55 歲。)

答案：(D)

14. W: Arthur can work out eight problems in ten minutes, Tony.

(女：亞瑟可以在十分鐘內計算八道題，東尼。)

M: Really? He can work faster than I. But Joyce can work out two more problems than Arthur in ten minutes.

(男：真的？他可以比我做得快。但是喬依絲在十分鐘內可以比亞瑟多計算兩道題。)

Question: How many problems can Joyce work out in ten minutes?

(問題：喬依絲十分鐘內可以計算幾道題？)

(A)12 problems. (12 題)　　　　　　　(B)8 problems. (8 題)

(C)10 problems (10 題)　　　　　　　(D)2 problems. (2 題)

答案：(C)

15. W: Have you finished all your homework? (女：你已經做完你全部的作業了？)

M: Sorry. I haven't finished my English homework. Instead I have finished my Chinese homework. I copied down the maths homework wrongly, so I did the wrong work.

（男：抱歉。我還沒做完我的英文作業。我反而做完了我的中文作業。我把數學作業抄錯了，所以我做錯作業了。）

Question: Which homework has the boy finished? (問題：這位男孩做完了哪一科的作業？)

(A)His Chinese homework. (他的中文作業)　　(B)His English homework. (她的英文作業)

(C)His maths homework. (她的數學作業)　　　(D)None. (都沒做)

答案：(A)

16. W: Did you learn English last night? (女：你昨晚有念英文嗎？)

M: Yes, I did. And I also watched TV at the same time. (男：有，我有。我還同時看了電視。)

W: It sounds a little strange. How could you do that? (女：這聽起來有點怪。你怎麼能做到？)

M: It was quite easy. I watched the programme in English on Channel 9.

（男：頗簡單的。我看了一個第九台的英文節目。）

Question: What did the man do last night? (問題：這位男士昨晚做了什麼？)

(A)He watched TV. (他看電視。)

(B)He learned English by watching TV. (他透過看電視學英文。)

(C)He learned English and then watched TV. (他先學英文再看電視。)

(D)He learned English. (他學英文。)

答案：(B)

Ⅲ、Listen to the passage and decide whether the following statements are True (T) or False (F).

● Oceans cover 2/3 of Earth, but ocean water is salty. In fact, most of the water in the world is not drinkable!

海洋覆蓋了地球的三分之二，但是海水是鹹的。事實上，世界上大部分的水都不能喝！

● Ground water is drinkable, but it is very easy to pollute it. For example, 4.

5 litres of paint or about 1 litre of oil can get into the ground and pollute 1,125,000 litres of drinking water!

地下水可以喝，但它很容易被污染。舉例來說，四點五公升油漆或大約一公升油可以進入土地而污染一百一十二萬五千公升飲用水！

● If a broken tap can fill up a coffee cup in 10 minutes, it will waste over 13,500 litres of water in a year. How much water is that? You would have to drink 65 glasses of water every day for a year to get that much water!

如果一個壞掉的水龍頭可以在十分鐘注滿一個咖啡杯，它一年可以浪費一萬三千五百公升的水。這是多少水呢？你要每天喝六十五杯的水喝一年才有那麼多水！

● If you leave the water running while you brush your teeth, you might waste 22.5 litres of water each time. That is enough to fill 65 soft drink cans!

如果你在刷牙的時候讓水繼續流，你可能每次浪費二十二點五公升的水。那足夠注滿六十五個飲料罐。

● If you leave the water running while you wash the dishes, you might waste 135 litres of water each time — enough to wash a whole car!

如果你洗碗的時候讓水繼續流，你可能每次浪費一百三十五公升的水－足夠洗一整輛車。

● Believe it or not, the water in our toilets starts as fresh water! Each time you flush the toilet, it uses 18 to 31.5 litres of fresh water.

信不信由你，在你的馬桶裡的水一開始是清水！每次你沖馬桶，它用掉十八至三十一點五公升清水。

● A shower usually takes at least 5 minutes. You could use 50 litres of water taking one shower. In a year, that is almost 18,000 litres of water!

淋浴通常需要至少五分鐘。你一次淋浴可以用掉五十公升的水。一年之中，那幾乎是一萬八千公升的水！

● Taking a bath uses even more water than showers — about twice as much. Every time you take a bath you can easily use 120 to 160 litres of water.

泡澡甚至比淋浴使用更多水－大約兩倍之多。每次你泡一個澡你可以輕易用掉一百二十至一百六十公升的水。

17. Drinking water can be easily polluted and even a litre of oil can pollute 11,250,000 litres of drinking water.

(飲用水很容易被污染而僅僅一公升的油可以污染一千兩百五十萬公升的飲用水。)

答案：(F 錯)

18. 13,500 litres of water equals to the amount that you drink 56 glasses of water every day for a year. (一萬三千五百公升的水等於你每天飲用五十六杯水持續一年。)

答案：(F 錯)

19. 65 soft drink cans can hold about 22.5 litres of water.

(六十五個飲料罐可裝大約二十二點五公升的水。)

答案：(T 對)

20. According to the speaker, 135 litres of water is enough to wash a whole car.

(根據講者，一百三十五公升的水足夠洗一整輛車。)

答案：(T 對)

21. It seems that the water we use to flush toilets each time is of about 80 litres.

(似乎我們每次用來沖馬桶的水大約是八十公升。)

答案：(F 錯)

22. It saves water if you take a shower rather than a bath. (如果你淋浴而不泡澡會節省水。)

答案：(T 對)

23. The passage tells us some facts about using water. (此短文告訴我們一些使用水方面的真相。)

答案：(T 對)

What can we do?
我們能做什麼？

We can do many things to keep water clean. We can stop polluting water in our daily life.

我們可以做很多事情來維持水清潔。我們可以在我們的日常生活中停止污染水。

Whenever you see litter, such as cans, plastic bags and cigarette butts, on the street, pick it up. When rainwater washes over this litter, it becomes polluted. This polluted water flows into rivers and the sea.

任何時候當你看到垃圾，例如金屬罐、塑膠袋和菸蒂，在街道上，把它撿起來。當雨水沖刷過這些垃圾，它就被污染了。這個汙染的水流入河川和大海。

Do not throw paint, oil or litter down your sink or toilet. Pick up your dog's droppings. When they are washed into water in rivers or the sea, they increase bacteria levels.

不要丟棄油漆、油或垃圾到你的水槽或馬桶裡。撿起你的狗的糞便。當它們被沖入水中進入河流或大海，它們會增加細菌量。

Take household chemicals, waste oil, etc., to the specific sections of official landfills.

把家庭用的化學藥品、廢油等等拿去的官方指定地的特別區域。

Do not throw litter on nearby beaches. We can organize a project with our school or join a community group to help clean the beaches instead.

不要在附近的海灘丟垃圾。反而，我們可以和學校組織一個專案或參加社會團體來幫助清潔海灘。

- Pick up litter like __24__, __25__ bags and cigarette ends before rainwater washes it over.
  (在雨水沖刷它們之前，把例如金屬罐、塑膠袋和菸蒂撿起來。)
- Don't throw __26__, __27__ or litter down your sink or toilet.
  (不要丟棄油漆、油或垃圾到你的水槽或馬桶裡。)
- Pick up your dog's __28__.
  (撿起你的狗的糞便。)
- Take household __29__, waste oil to the specific sections of official landfills.
  (把家庭用的化學藥品、廢油拿到官方指定地的特別區域。)
- Do not throw litter on nearby __30__.
  (不要在附近的海灘丟垃圾。)

24. 答案：cans
25. 答案：plastic
26. 答案：paint
27. 答案：oil
28. 答案：droppings
29. 答案：chemicals2
30. 答案：beaches

全新英語聽力測驗【八年級/高階版(下)】

出版者：建如資訊股份有限公司

　　　　夏朵文理補習班

發行：禾耘圖書文化有限公司

地址：新北市新店區安祥路 109 巷 15 號

電話：02-29422385　傳真：02-29426087

劃撥帳號：50231111 禾耘圖書文化有限公司

總經銷：紅螞蟻圖書有限公司

地址：台北市 114 內湖區舊宗路 2 段 121 巷 28 號 4 樓

網站：www.e-redant.com

電話：02-27953656 傳真：02-27954100

劃撥帳號：16046211 紅螞蟻圖書有限公司

ISBN：978-986-88584-3-5

出版日期:103 年 7 月

本書由華東師範大學出版社有限公司授權夏朵文理補習班

及建如資訊股份有限公司出版發行。

定價 400 元

筆 記 欄

筆記欄

筆 記 欄

筆記欄

筆 記 欄

筆記欄

夏朵英文